The
Souls
of
Animals

The Souls of Animals

Gary A. Kowalski

With photographs by Art Wolfe

✳ STILLPOINT PUBLISHING
Walpole, New Hampshire

✳ STILLPOINT PUBLISHING

Books that explore the expanding frontiers
of human consciousness

For a free catalog or ordering information, write:
Stillpoint Publishing, PO Box 640, Walpole, NH 03608, USA
or TOLL-FREE 800-847-4014 (Continental USA only)
or 603-756-9281 (Foreign, and Alaska and Hawaii)

This book is manufactured in the United States of America.

Cover Design by Karen Savary
Text design by Heather Gendron

Published by Stillpoint Publishing,
a division of Stillpoint International, Inc.,
Box 640, Meetinghouse Road, Walpole, NH 03608

Library of Congress Catalog Card Number: 98-061468

Kowalski, Gary A.
The Souls of Animals
ISBN 1-883478-21-9

2 3 4 5 6 7 8 9 0

This book is printed on acid-free recycled paper
to save trees and preserve Earth's ecology.

We should understand well that all things are the works of the Great Spirit. We should know the Great Spirit is within all things: the trees, the grasses, the rivers, the mountains, and the four-legged and winged peoples; and even more important, we should understand that the Great Spirit is also above all these things and peoples. When we do understand all this deeply in our hearts, then we will fear, and love, and know the Great Spirit, and then we will be and act and live as the Spirit intends.

—BLACK ELK

The author invites readers to share their own
experiences that illuminate the souls of animals.
Please send your stories to:

Rev. Gary Kowalski
c/o The First Unitarian Universalist Society
152 Pearl Street
Burlington, Vermont 05401

Contents

Photographs

By Art Wolfe

Acknowledgements

I wish to thank all those who have supplied information and inspiration for *The Souls of Animals*. I am especially grateful to the thousands of people who have read the first edition of the book and to the dozens who have written me letters, sharing their stories and thanking me for confirming their own conviction that animals do indeed have souls. I have tried to answer and acknowledge each of these messages. Many of the letters have given me new insight as well as material for this revised edition.

I remain indebted to Art Wolfe for the stunning photographs that are part of this book, to Karen Savary for the beautiful cover design, and to Errol Sowers, Dorothy Mills, and Meredith Young-Sowers of Stillpoint Publishing, for their enthusiasm and their numerous recommendations for improvements in my manuscript.

I must also say thank you to Tom Regan, Professor of Philosophy at North Carolina State University, for writing the foreword to this revision. Professor Regan has been an inspiration not only to me but to a whole generation of students and activists who have been influenced by his clear thinking and passionate commitment to animal rights.

I wish to express my appreciation to Elmer Fisk for permission to retell the story of Boob, the dog who believed in ghosts; to the Gorilla Foundation for permission to reprint the conversation between Koko and Maureen Sheehan concerning death, which appears in Chapter Two; and to W.W. Norton Publishers for permission to reprint extracts from *To Whom It May Concern: An Investigation of the Art of Elephants.*

In addition to the sources listed in the chapter notes, many others provided factual information for *The Souls of Animals.* These include Professor Jeannette Haviland of Rutgers University, who directed me to research on the development of self-concept in infancy; Gordon Dietzman and Scott Swengel of the International Crane Foundation, who gave me updates on the fortunes of Tex, Faith, and Gee Whiz; and Hank Kite, who read "Hearts of Song" and suggested additions to the text. Dr. Roger Fouts of Central Washington University shared as yet unpublished information about Moja's artwork. Thanks go also to Margaret Carter for her amazing animal stories and to Timothy Grannis for his thoughts on art.

I am grateful as well to my good friends John Kern and Valerie Hurley for their editorial advice and personal support. Finally, no list of acknowledgement would be complete without mentioning my wife, Dori Jones, who reads almost everything I write and offers kind but honest criticism. Thankfully, she has good taste in books and men.

Foreword

What a piece of work we humans are! So unsure are we of our place in the grand scheme of things, we even enlist our language to mask our cosmic *angst*. On one side of the semantic ledger we find the word *animal;* on the other side, the word *human*. That humans are animals, it seems, is a troubling fact we would like to forget. After all, no self-respecting human would want to be caught "acting like an animal."

This denial of our animality has had predictable consequences. To begin with, it has nurtured centuries of ignorance about our brothers and sisters in fur, and feather, and fin. One rarely explores what one "knows" isn't worth exploring in the first place. No one should be surprised, therefore, when (as is true of the dominant traditions in the western world) other-than-human animals are viewed as inferior beings having no purpose beyond serving the interests of the master species: *Homo sapiens*. Chimpanzees belong in biomedical research labs, don't they? A pig's reason for being is as ham, between two slices of bread, isn't it? What could be clearer than that?

Part of the strength of the restrained, graceful words we read on these pages can be traced to Gary Kowalski's gentle yet resolute assault on this shameful record of our species' hubris. What place does our vaunted "superiority" have when we read that gorillas grieve the loss of friends; elephants attempt to comfort kin who are dying; young birds need to be taught what to sing; African wild dogs risk their own lives to save that of a pup; dolphins, orcas, and whooping cranes frolic for the sheer fun of it; and both geese and jackdaws mate for life?

Because we have viewed other animals through the myopic lens of our self-importance, we have misperceived who and what they are. Because we have repeated our ignorance, one to the other, we have mistaken it for knowledge. It takes no special training to recognize how little one knows. It does take a special kind of wisdom to acknowledge and overcome it. As he demonstrates on every page of this book, Gary Kowalski is among the very few who are wise.

Earlier, I noted that our species' hubris has infected how we understand other animals. Not surprisingly, our shared arrogance has also encouraged widespread misconceptions about who and what we are. Steeped in the traditions of denial, we humans have wanted to view ourselves as being in the world, but not of it—

alive within the larger community of life, but not an equal member in it.

If Gary Kowalski has his way, this all-too-familiar fantasy will not long endure. Since other-than-human animals really are so much like us, how can we be so much better than they? Since they not only are in the world, but of the world, how can we plausibly continue to view ourselves as apart from, not as a part of, the city of life?

"We are the youngest siblings in life's family — the perpetual neonates of the animal world," Gary Kowalski writes near this book's end. "In a fundamental way we need other creatures to tell us who we are." Whether or not we learn from these, our neglected tutors, this much we know: all animals are fortunate to have Gary Kowalski as our shared ambassador, creating the cognitive space in which other animals can speak the truths they know, preparing the spiritual place for us to hear them.

—TOM REGAN

PUBLISHER'S NOTE:
Tom Regan is a Professor and Department Head for the Department of Philosophy and Religion at North Carolina State University.

For ancient peoples, the soul was located in the breath or the blood. For me, soul resides at the point where our lives intersect with the timeless, in our love of goodness, our passion for beauty, our quest for meaning and truth. In asking whether animals have souls, we are inquiring whether they share in the qualities that make life more than a mere struggle for survival, endowing existence with dignity and élan.

1

Do Animals Have Souls?
What is the Question?

Imagine a warm spring day on a small farm in Mississippi. The flowers are in fragrant bloom, and a sow that has free run of the farmyard has just given birth to piglets. Later that day, a glance under the porch where the new babies are resting reveals a wonderful sight. The mother pig has carefully bitten off blossoms to make a bouquet of jonquils, which she has arranged in a bright yellow wreath surrounding the sleeping litter.

No one who saw such a scene could doubt that animals know just as much about nurturing and celebrating life as people do, and maybe much more. The woman who wrote to tell me about this barnyard nativity accompanied her letter with a hand-rendered drawing showing a halo of flowers with their stems pointing outward, petals toward the center, piglets nestled snugly in the middle. She included other stories as well, like the one about her two horses Rifle, a gelding, and April, a pretty black mare. Rifle was quite enamored of April. When the mare was sent to Missouri to be bred to a race horse, Rifle was never the same again, and he died not long afterward. Such experiences, along with seventy-four years of caring for dogs and cats, convinced my correspondent that animals indeed have souls, with joys and sorrows very much like our own.

Over the years I received a good many letters like that from readers who believed, like me, that animals can inspire us to wiser and more winsome living. When *The Souls of Animals* was first published, I wrote about my own dog, Chinook, calling him my spiritual guide. Although he is no longer living, what I said then still holds:

> *"My dog has deep knowledge to impart. He makes friends easily and doesn't hold a grudge. He enjoys simple pleasures and takes each day as it comes. Like a true Zen master, he eats when he's hungry and sleeps when he's tired. He's not hung up about sex. Best of all, he befriends me with an unconditional love that human beings would do well to emulate.*
>
> *"Chinook does have his failings, of course. He's afraid of firecrackers and hides in the clothes closet whenever we run the vacuum cleaner, but unlike me he's not afraid of what other people think of him or anxious about his public image. He barks at the mail carrier and*

the newsboy, but in contrast with some people I know he never growls at the children or barks at his wife.

"So my dog is a sort of guru. When I become too serious and preoccupied, he reminds me of the importance of frolicking and play. When I get too wrapped up in abstractions and ideas, he reminds me of the importance of exercising and caring for my body. On his own canine level, he shows me that it might be possible to live without inner conflicts or neuroses: uncomplicated, genuine, and glad to be alive."

As Mark Twain remarked long ago, human beings have a lot to learn from the Higher Animals. Just because they haven't invented static cling, ICBMs, or television evangelists doesn't mean they aren't spiritually evolved.

But what does it mean for an animal (including the human animal) to be spiritually evolved? In my mind, it means many things: the development of a moral sense, the appreciation of beauty, the capacity for creativity, and the awareness of one's self within a larger universe as well as a sense of mystery and wonder about it all. These are the most precious gifts we possess, yet there is nothing esoteric or otherworldly about such spiritual capabilities. Indeed, my contention is that spirituality is quite natural, rooted firmly in the biological order and in the ecology shared by all life.

This book is about the spiritual lives of animals: whooping cranes, elephants, jackdaws, gorillas, songbirds, horses, and household dogs and cats. Much has been written about the intelligence of other species and their ability to solve problems. But spirituality is related less to problem-solving than to the kinds of problems we are even able to consider. We may contemplate death, for instance, without ever really hoping to "solve" the problem of our own demise. In reflecting on the spiritual lives of other creatures, therefore, I am concerned less with raw brain power, memory, and learning ability than I am with more subtle facets of intellgience such as empathy, artistry, and imagination.

Investigations of interspecies spirituality take us into unmapped territory. Are other animals conscious of themselves, as we are? Do they grieve or have thoughts and feelings about the end of life? Do animals dream? Do they have a conscience or a sense of right and wrong? Do other species make music or appreciate art?

In the years that have passed since this book first appeared, more and more experts have begun to address questions like these. A well-known psychologist has published a work on the emotional lives of animals: *When Elephants Weep.* Frans de Waal, a noted primatologist, has written books on peacemaking among primates and on the ways the political manuevering of chimps often seems to mirror our own. I am glad that these issues are finally receiving more attention from reputable researchers and scientists. Indeed, this book could not have been written without the insights of pioneers like Jane Goodall and Konrad Lorenz. Since I am not a zoologist, I depend heavily on their data. But while I have striven to be accurate and objective in my findings, this is a book that has more to do with religion than with science.

I am a parish minister by vocation, so my own field of expertise is in the realm of the intangible. I pray with the dying and counsel the bereaved. I christen infants, and share in the joy of parents when new life comes into the world. I occasionally help people think through moral quandaries and make ethical decisions, and I also share a responsibilty for educating the young, helping them realize their inborn potential for reverence and compassion. Week after week I stand before my congregation and try to talk about the unfathomed riddles of existence. While I do not claim to know all the answers, having the title "Reverend" in front of my name does permit me to raise a host of questions that might be considered off-limits by hard-headed scientists and academicians. Clergy have a professional license to ponder topics that others consider imponderable.

As late twentieth-century shamans, we are allowed to examine enigmas like "What makes us human?" and "What makes life sacred?" We can ask not only about the mating behavior and survival strategies of other animals but whether they have souls and spirits like our own. The danger here is that we are often in over our heads. But at least we are swimming in deep water and out of the shallows. In searching for answers to such queries, I have found, we not only enrich our understanding of other creatures, we also gain insight into ourselves.

Without anthropomorphizing our nonhuman relations we can acknowledge that animals share many human characteristics. They have individual likes and dislikes, moods and mannerisms, and possess their own integrity, which suffers when not respected. They play and are curious about their world. They develop friendships and sometimes risk their own lives to help others. They have "animal faith," a spontaneity and directness that can be most refreshing.

To me, animals have all the traits indicative of soul. For soul is not something we can see or measure. We can observe only its outward manifestations: in tears and laughter, in courage and heroism, in generosity and forgiveness. Soul is what's behind-the-scenes in the tough and tender moments when we are most intensely and grippingly alive. But what exactly is the soul? Since *The Souls of Animals* first came to print, a great deal has been written on that subject. Bookstores now have shelves bursting with titles like *Care of the Soul* and *Chicken Soup for the Soul* (in multiple servings). Having been neglected and almost lost for many years, the term *soul* is currently in danger of becoming clichéd through overuse. That would be a shame, for *soul* is a rich and resonant word that needs to be reclaimed and, perhaps, redefined.

Many people think of soul as the element of personality that survives bodily death, but for me it refers to something much more down-to-earth. Soul is the marrow of our existence as sentient, sensitive beings. It's soul that's revealed in great works of art, and soul that's lifted up in awe when we stand in silence under a night sky burning with billions of stars. When we speak of a soulful piece of music, we mean one that comes out of infinite depths of feeling. When we speak of the soul of a nation, we mean its capacity for valor and visionary change. "The soul," said the psychoanalyst Carl Jung, "is partly in eternity and partly in time." Soul is present wherever our lives intersect the dimension of the holy: in moments of intimacy, in flights of fancy, and in rituals that hallow the evanescent events of our lives with enduring significance. Soul is what makes each of our lives a microcosm—not merely a meaningless fragment of the universe, but at some level a reflection of the whole.

No one can prove that animals have souls. Asking for proof would be like demanding proof that I love my wife and children, or wanting me to prove that Handel's *Messiah* is a glorious masterpiece of music. Some truths simply cannot be demonstrated. But if we open our hearts to other creatures and allow ourselves to sympathize with their joys and struggles, we will find they have the power to touch and transform us. There is an inwardness in other creatures that awakens what is innermost in ourselves.

For ages people have known that animals have a balance and harmony we can learn from. Their instincts and adaptations to life are sometimes healthier than our own. "In the beginning of all things," said the Pawnee Chief Letakots-Lesa, "wisdom and knowledge were with the animals." The Pawnee believed that "Tirawa, the One Above," did not speak directly to human beings but sent certain animals as messengers and healers, and that humans should learn from them as well as from the stars, the sun, and the moon. Other creatures have inhabited the earth much longer than we have, and as native peoples realized, they have much to teach us about our world.

This book is devoted to exploring the extent to which animals can be our guides, soul mates and fellow travelers, sharing in the things that make us most deeply human. Each chapter looks at a different facet of animal experience. Why do animals play? What are their fears and fantasies? What does the world look like through their eyes? How close are their experiences to our own?

A work like this may raise more questions than it answers. Yet if the questions serve to make us more appreciative of the other creatures who share this planet, the book will have served its purpose. For I believe that if we are to keep our family homestead— third stone from the sun—safe for coming generations, we must awaken to a new respect for the family of life.

Those of us alive today are witnesses and accomplices to an extintinction of the earth's inhabitants unlike any known in previous human history. Millions of species are at risk. Yet as animal rights activist and author Alice Walker reminds us, "anything we love can be saved." In asking if animals have souls, we are also asking whether we can learn to care about them passionately enough to insure their future . . . and our own.

Thankfully, more and more people are becoming concerned for other species—one additional reason for an updated version of this book. In a poll of more than a thousand Americans conducted in 1996 by the Associated Press, two thirds of those questioned agreed with the premise that "an animal's right to live free of suffering should be just as important as a person's." The same number believed it was wrong to use animals in cosmetics testing, while a majority disapproved of killing them for their fur or in hunting for sport. In America, as elsewhere, attitudes are changing. The more we learn about other creatures, in their richness and complexity, the more people come to realize the preciousness of life in all its forms.

Frequently, it is one particular animal that opens our hearts. For me, it was my dog Chinook, who was twelve when he lay down last summer for the final time. Now that I have a galloping, bouncing puppy in the house, I realize that Chinook was an "old soul" even as a youngster: considerate, calm, even-tempered, and gentle. But while Chinook was a remarkable animal, I also realize that he was far from being unique. The world is full of astonishing creatures, each with a gift to share and a lesson to impart. Is it possible, I wonder, to embrace all of creation—the insects, the birds, the plants, wild creatures and tame ones—with a degree of the same doting fondness I felt for that wise, sweet-natured old dog? If I can learn to love that much, then there's hope for me, and maybe hope for us all.

Life is filled with grief. Death and loss are unavoidable companions of the flesh. But are we the only animals who grieve? Do other creatures have thoughts and feelings about the end of life or wonder what lies beyond? The consciousness of our own mortality is part of what makes us human—it is one of the elements that makes us a spiritual animal—but it may be an aspect of life we share with many other species.

2

Mortals All

Are Animals Aware of Death?

It's always hard to say good-bye. As a parish minister, part of my job is caring for the dying and bereaved, but finding the right words doesn't get any easier with practice. What do you say to the parents whose one-day-old daughter—their first child—died because she was born with part of her heart missing? What do you say at a memorial service for a middle-aged man, a cancer victim, that will give solace and support to his widow and two teenagers? Words aren't adequate to address the shock and desolation we feel when a loved one dies.

The only thing that seems to help is a caring presence. So we gather with our families. Our friends come around. We assemble in our spiritual communities. We light a candle, share a hug, or join in a moment of silence. And although we don't stop grieving, we know that we don't grieve alone. Others, who have also borne tragedy in their lives, understand the pain we feel. And out of that shared suffering we somehow gather strength to endure the loss.

Do other animals feel grief? We know that people grieve for their pets, of course. People in my congregation have come to me many times for counseling when their animal companions die. The loss of a beloved dog or cat can be very upsetting and naturally makes us sad. But I was stunned the first time I heard about Koko, the gorilla who grieved for her pet kitten. Koko's story convinced me that animals, like people, also have strong feelings about the end of life.

Koko is a female lowland gorilla who for more than two decades has been the focus of the world's longest ongoing ape language study.[1] Instead of using spoken words, Koko communicates in Ameslan, or American Sign Language. Her teacher, Dr. Francine "Penny" Patterson of the California Gorilla Foundation, has helped the ape master a vocabulary of more than five hundred words. That's how Koko told Penny she wanted a cat for her birthday. She signs the word cat by drawing two fingers across her cheeks to indicate whiskers.

One day a litter of three kittens was brought to the rural compound in Woodside, California, where Koko lives. The kittens had been abandoned at birth. Their "foster mother" was a terrier, who suckled them through the first month of life. Handling them with the gentle behavior typical of gorillas, Koko chose her pet, a tailless kitten with grey fur. She named her young friend "All Ball."

Koko enjoyed her new kitten, sniffing it and stroking it tenderly. She carried All Ball tucked against her upper leg and attempted to nurse it as if it were a baby gorilla. Koko was surprised to learn that kittens bite. When All Ball bit her on the finger, she made the signs for "dirty" and "toilet," her usual expressions of disapproval. It wasn't long, though, before Koko was signing the cat to tickle her—one of the gorilla's favorite games. "Koko seems to think that cats can do most things that she can do," said Penny.

"Soft/good/cat," said Koko.

One night All Ball escaped from the Gorilla Foundation and was accidentally killed by a car. When Koko was told about the accident, she at first acted as if she didn't hear or understand. Then a few minutes later she started to cry with high-pitched sobs. "Sad/frown" and "Sleep/cat" were her responses when the kitten was mentioned later. For nearly a week after the loss Koko cried whenever the subject of cats came up.

The gorilla clearly missed her feline companion. But how much did she understand about what had happened? Fortunately, it was possible to ask Koko directly. Maureen Sheehan, a staff member at the Gorilla Foundation, interviewed Koko about her thoughts on death.

"Where do gorillas go when they die?" Maureen asked.

Koko replied, "Comfortable/hole/bye [the sign for kissing a person good-bye]."

"When do gorillas die?" she asked.

Koko replied with the signs "Trouble/old."

"How do gorillas feel when they die: happy, sad, afraid?"

"Sleep," answered Koko.[2]

Gorillas not only mourn. Like human beings, they seem able to reflect on their own demise and struggle with the same sorts of questions that haunt us when a loved one dies.

All living things die, but it has long been assumed that only humans have any consciousness of this. It is a commonplace among philosophers that humankind is the only animal for whom death is an intellectual and emotional "problem." In his Pulitzer Prize-winning book, *The Denial of Death*, philosopher Ernest Becker draws the distinction between all other creatures, who "live in a tiny world, a sliver of reality, one neuro-chemical program that keeps them walking behind their nose and shuts out everything else," and *Homo sapiens*, "an animal who has no defense against full perception of the external world, an animal completely open to experience."[3]

Our power of memory and foresight, according to Becker and other philosophers, gives human beings a position in the universe that is both exalted and tragic. Our superior intellect enables us to look beyond the present moment to contemplate endless vistas of times past and eons to come. We gaze through telescopes and witness the birth of stars; we study fossils that tell of drifting continents and life forms long extinct. From this elevated vantage, however, we foresee the inevitability of death and ask what meaning our brief lives have in the vast panorama of existence.

The awareness of death is what makes human life so bittersweet and poignant, and it is this awareness, say those like Becker, that sets us apart from all other creatures. Knowledge of our own mortality is what makes us a spiritual animal. Where do we find faith and strength to live, knowing that death awaits us? What gives meaning and purpose to our days, knowing that our days so soon come to an end? Our answers may differ, but no one can ignore such questions. They are religious questions, and they are an inescapable part of being human.

But is *Homo sapiens* the only species that possesses the consciousness of death? There is much evidence that we are not alone in this regard.

Not only gorillas but also elephants may share in this awareness. Cynthia Moss, Director of the Amboseli Elephant Research Project in Kenya, has for more than a dozen years studied the lives of African elephants. While uprooting the time-worn myth of the "elephants' graveyard," her research suggests that these animals do appear to have some awareness of death, feelings of grief, and perhaps what might even be construed as funerary rituals.[4]

The legend of the elephants' graveyard probably arose because elephants that are sick or wounded tend to congregate in areas where there is water, shade, and good vegetation. Such a site might contain an unusually large number of elephant carcasses, Moss explains, giving rise to the graveyard fable. But while they don't have a graveyard, elephants do seem to have some notion of death.

Unlike most other animals, elephants recognize the dead bodies or skeletons of their own kind. When an elephant encounters another's corpse, he or she explores the body carefully and inquisitively with feet and trunk, smelling it and feeling the shape of the skull and tusks, perhaps in an effort to recognize the individual that has died. Even a bare and sun-bleached skeleton will elicit the interest of other elephants, who inevitably stop to inspect the bones, turning them with their trunks, picking them up and carrying them from one place to another, as though trying to find a proper "resting place" for the remains.

Even more striking is the elephant's response when a family member dies. Because elephants live almost as long as people (the oldest elephant in captivity died at the age of seventy-one), the bonds they form are lasting.

In 1977 one of the family groups Moss studied was attacked by hunters. An animal that Moss named Tina, a young female about fifteen years old, was shot in the chest, the bullet penetrating her right lung. With the larger herd in panicky flight, Tina's immediate family slowed to help her, crowding about her as the blood poured from her mouth. As the groaning elephant began to slump to the ground, her mother, Teresia, and Trista, another older female, positioned themselves on each side, leaning inward to support her weight and hold her upright. But their efforts were to no avail. With a great shudder Tina collapsed and died.

Teresia and Trista tried frantically to resuscitate the dead animal, kicking and tusking her and attempting to raise her body from the earth. Tallulah, another member of the family, even tried stuffing a trunkful of grass into Tina's mouth. Tina's mother, with great difficulty, lifted the limp body with her mighty tusks. Then, with a sharp crack, Teresia's tusk broke under the strain, leaving a jagged stub of ivory and bloody tissue.

The elephants refused to leave the body, however. They began to dig in the rocky dirt and, with their trunks, sprinkled soil over Tina's lifeless form. Some went into the brush and broke branches, which they brought back and placed on the carcass. By nightfall the body was nearly covered with branches and earth. Throughout the night members of the family stood in vigil over their fallen friend. Only as dawn began to break did they leave, heading back to the safety of the Amboseli reserve. Teresia, Tina's mother, was the last to go.

I have often watched people linger at the graveside after the ceremony of committal. The body has been returned to earth and the spirit commended to the keeping of God. The prayers have all been said and the last "Amen" has been uttered. Yet the family members remain by the grave, saying their final farewells. Perhaps elephants feel a similar reluctance to say good-bye to their loved ones. One mother elephant whose calf was stillborn stayed with the body four days, according to Moss, protecting it from lions and scavengers that lay in wait. Mothers who lose their calves can be lethargic for days afterward, she discovered, and the loss of a family matriarch can disrupt the social organization for long periods, sometimes permanently. It is not unscientific to suppose that elephants may experience shock and depression comparable to what human beings feel when a loved one dies.

Other eyewitnesses agree with that assessment. D.J. Schubert, who became well-acquainted with elephants while working in the Peace Corps in West Africa, once chanced upon a family of elephants surrounding a fallen infant. After long hours of trying to help the baby to its feet, the elders finally buried the corpse with dirt, grass, and leaves. Family members then continued to stand watch, slowly rocking their great bodies and comforting each other, intertwining their trunks and using that sensuous appendage to gently touch each other's mouthparts, seemingly in a kiss. "I had just witnessed an elephant funeral," Schubert says.[5] The Peace Corps volunteer was sleepless later that night, feeling bereft and alone, remembering the screams that had been exchanged between the mother and her sick, dying child. Who could doubt that the elephants themselves were also troubled and uneasy? As evening descended, the family with a baby missing must have known something of what religious people call "the dark night of the soul."

I feel a sense of compassion for Teresia and also for Koko, pained and at the same time comforted to realize that in thinking and wondering about death I am not alone. Koko's answers to the question "Where do gorillas go when they die?" are probably as good as yours or mine. None of us really knows what happens to people or primates or other living things when they die. One thing seems certain, however. All of us face the end of life with some of the same primary emotions. It is wrenching. It makes us sad. Although of different species we are not so separate as we seem.

I feel richer knowing that gorillas love—not just like human beings, but in their own meaningful way—and that elephants also share feelings of tenderness and grief—not just like ours, but not so different, either. Such knowledge reminds me that my own private loads of anguish and my own private moments of intimacy and joy are not so private after all. The realization that we share tears and affection tells me that you and I and Tina and All Ball are interconnected. We are part of a larger world: not an inert or unfeeling world but a world full of pain, healing, passion, and hope.

In such a world we find the consolation of companionship. As Helen Keller writes, "We bereaved are not alone. We belong to the largest company in all the world—the company of those who have known suffering." The company of the bereaved may be much larger than we once imagined. It may include not only gorillas and elephants but many others in the nonhuman realm whose thoughts and emotions about the end of life are similar to our own. A friend of mine who raised cattle on a small farm in Central America told me how one day a calf was slaughtered by a band of campesinos, who roasted the flesh for an impromptu fiesta. For weeks afterward, until the onset of the rainy season, the remainder of the herd gathered each afternoon and stood lowing in a circle around the spot where the young one had been butchered. How can we heedlessly take the life of another animal? How can we kill without wondering what agony that creature feels, or what heartbreak besets its mate and offspring? Knowing that our pain is shared might make us more careful, less callous, in our dealings with other creatures.

Concern for the distress of animals is a time-honored precept of many religious traditions. Accounts of elephants shedding tears can be traced all the way back to the Ramayana, one of the ancient scriptures of India, and *ahimsa*, the principle of non-injury toward other living things, has been a part of Hindu philosophy for thousands of years. Buddhists, similarly, vow to free all sentient beings from suffering. Jains refuse to kill even the smallest organism. Western religions have not always been so attuned to the plight of other creatures. Yet the prophet Mohammed is said to have awakened from his nap one afternoon to find a small, sick kitten sleeping on the edge of his cloak; he cut off his garment rather than disturb the pathetic creature. Hebrew scriptures contain numerous admonitions to care for creation, as in Deuteronomy, where the law forbids harnessing a bull and a donkey together, since "the weaker would suffer in trying to keep up with the stronger." In the New Testament, the apostle Paul tells us in characteristically mythic language that "the whole created universe groans in all its parts" under the burdens of suffering and death. Perhaps if we listen intently we can hear the groaning of the animals, who beg for our mercy and forbearance.

We are mortals all, human and nonhuman, bound in one fellowship of love and travail. No one escapes the fate of death. But we can, with caring, make our good-byes less tormented. If we broaden the circle of our compassion, life can be less cruel.

NOTES

1. Jane Vessels, "Koko's Kitten," *National Geographic*, Vol. 167, No. 1, p. 110.
2. Francine Patterson and Eugene Linden, *The Education of Koko* (New York: Holt, Rinehart & Winston, 1981), pp. 190-191.
3. Ernest Becker, *The Denial of Death* (New York: Macmillan, 1973), pp. 50-51.
4. Cynthia Moss, *Elephant Memories: Thirteen Years in the Life of an Elephant Family* (New York: William Morrow, 1988), pp. 72-74, 270-271.
5. Undated account by D.J. Schubert quoted in letter of Holly Cheever, D.V.M., to the author, March 9, 1996.

The universe is a wondrously strange and mystifying place. At times its very mystery makes us fearful, and we fill the dark unknown with phantoms and apparitions of our own imagining. Do other animals also have a sense of the mysterious? Like us, they inhabit a world that is often inexplicable. And their world, like ours, may occasionally contain hints and portents of the supernatural.

3

Ghosties, Goblins, and Four-Legged Beasties

Do Animals Have a Sense of the Mysterious?

I'm not sure whether or not I believe in ghosts, but like a lot of people, I get goosebumps when things happen that I can't explain. While I tend to be skeptical of the paranormal, I know enough people who have had strange experiences (many of them involving animals) to raise questions in my mind.

There were the lions my mother heard in Rome, for instance. It was her first trip to Europe, and she along with her two traveling companions had taken a cab straight from the airport for a late check-in at their hotel. In the morning, she complained of sleeplessness. "Did you hear the lions roaring?" she asked her friends.

The growling had kept her up most of the night. The others looked mystified. Neither one had heard anything, and Martin, who had visited the city many times, knew there were no zoos or circuses in the vicinity. Then his eyebrows shot up. "Do you realize," he asked, "that we are less than a block from the Coliseum?" His implication was that the roaring came from the wild beasts that were part of the gladiatorial games hundreds of years ago. Part of me would like to think there were simpler explanations. But another part will always wonder what my mother really heard that night.

Then there was the peculiar incident involving a household pet, an orange cat named Oro, that I learned about from a correspondent living in South Carolina. The family had just moved to a new home, and Oro seemed to adapt quite well, with a single queer exception. While she made herself perfectly at home everywhere else in the house, Oro always leaped when she had to cross the threshold between the living and dining rooms. After the family had been settled in their new house for a few months, the previous owners came calling. In the course of conversation, they mentioned how their old dog had loved to sleep on that particular threshold. Many years before, he had died in that house. Was there a faint scent remaining in the doorway, or did the cat sense the dog's lingering presence on some more subtle level? I am sure I will never know the answer.

I had the same bemused reaction in the first church I served, where there was a ghost named Walt. A number of people had seen him. Before he died, Walt had been a member of the congregation, but always kind of a loner. When Walt learned he had a terminal illness, he and the other members of the church began a journey of growth and discovery as they faced the crisis together. It was an opportunity to confront fears and explore feelings that had never been shared. In the process, many grew closer than ever before in their relationships with each other. After Walt died, some of those who had been nearest to him could still feel his presence in the church building. Two or three heard his voice there. Others saw his shadowy form on the edge of their field of vision, but before they could turn to look right at him, he had disappeared around a corner. I began to hear these ghost stories shortly after I arrived as the new pastor. I wasn't sure what to make of them, but they made me a little nervous. The folks in my congregation were mostly college-educated, like me, and weren't supposed to be "superstitious." In my three years at Harvard Divinity School, nothing had prepared me for spooks.

As I gained more experience in ministry, however, I learned that such experiences are fairly common. A high percentage of women who lose their husbands, for instance, report that they hear the voices of their departed spouses or see them in the days and weeks following their death. If we like, we can call these experiences hallucinations or products of the subconscious. Or we may speculate that the unconscious is a channel that taps into a different plane of reality. Whichever interpretation you prefer, it can be said that from a clinical standpoint such experiences are quite normal. There is a "superstitious" streak in all of us.

I have had some spine-tingling encounters of my own, but most of them turn out to have fairly simple explanations. One night, for instance, my wife and I awoke with a start when we heard a ghastly noise. A weird, wailing howl was rising from the foot of our bed. Rubbing the sleep and terror out of our eyes, we saw it was only our dog, deep in the land of dreams. Neither of us had ever heard him howl like that before, but apparently some unconscious memory had been released, maybe from the days when his great-grandsire was a wolf or his grandam a sled dog in the arctic.

As far as we know, most birds and mammals dream, or at least exhibit the pattern of rapid eye movement associated in human beings with dreaming. (The spiny anteater, for some peculiar reason, is an exception.) REM sleep is generated by the brainstem, an older section of the brain located just above the spinal cord that is shared by all vertebrates; maybe frogs and fish dream, too. Direct evidence of dreaming is hard to come by, but birds that mimic, such as parrots and mynah birds, have been reported to talk in their sleep.

Like many other dog owners, I've often watched my pet lying on the floor with his eyes closed, paws twitching, lips curled back and ears cocked, as though chasing some imaginary squirrel down the trails of night.

No one knows for sure what other animals are dreaming, but if they are like us their inner worlds may be filled with strange visions, fears, and fantasies. Scientists who study animal behavior seem to assume that animals' intelligence must always be concentrated on practical matters, like gathering food, finding mates, or escaping enemies. Yet we know that human consciousness includes much that is not practical or grounded in the hard light of reality. Our minds are also inhabited by shades and shadows: spirits, specters, and unearthly visitations.

Perhaps animals share with us some sense of the "supernatural." One member of my church, for instance, is convinced that his dog believes in ghosts.

As Elmer Fisk tells the story, he and his family were getting ready to move to a new home, sorting through their household possessions in preparation for the van coming the next morning. Late at night, he went to the dump with what was supposed to be the final load of last-minute junk. Included in the trash was a papier-mâché head that one of his children had made for the previous Halloween. According to Elmer's description, "It was just under life-size and had a lumpy, sickly, greenish complexion, with spent flash bulbs for eyes.

It was quite horrible." He decided the head had one more scare left in it, so instead of tossing it onto the pile, he positioned it carefully behind a fresh mound of coal ashes so it appeared to be sneaking a peek over the top.

Meanwhile, more debris had accumulated back at the house, necessitating yet another trip to the dump. This time the dog, who was named Boob, begged to go along.

In spite of his humble moniker, Boob was a highly intelligent animal, Elmer tells me, a Border Collie with wide-set eyes and long brown-and-white fur. Elmer was surprised, therefore, at what this sensible dog did when it saw the grotesque little man peeping over the pile of ashes.

> Boob saw it as soon as I did and reacted in a way that I had never seen him behave before. All his back hair rose up, his lips drew back from his fangs, and a low moan sounded in his throat while he trembled so badly that he shook the car. Boob was not the bravest of dogs (he was scared to death of any sharp noise, from thunder to the explosion of a cap gun), but I think if that had been a bear in the dump, or a lion even, he would have torn the door off the car to go after it. This was different. Whatever Boob thought he saw it was obviously beyond anything he

had encountered in his previous experience and therefore something beyond nature, or, if you will, super-natural. Boob never took his eyes off The Thing and was still craning his neck to keep it in sight as we made the turn toward home. When he could no longer see it, relief was written all over him.

Before laughing or feeling superior, ask yourself whether you would have reacted any differently. If I had been in that junkyard, I probably would have been as scared as that poor Border Collie! Psychologists have discovered that fear of the dark (and presumably fear of the nameless threats lurking there) is one of the few emotions that seem instinctive or innate to the human race. So while I don't necessarily believe in goblins or ghouls, some deep-seated part of me still cringes when things creak and go bump in the night. However educated or enlightened we fancy ourselves, all of us are afraid of the unknown.

This chilling sensation is different from ordinary fear, since it has no rational basis. It is more akin to awe than to simple apprehension. In his book *The Idea of the Holy*, the philosopher Rudolf Otto suggests that this sense of the uncanny, the eerie, the weird is the primal spiritual experience. At times we feel we are in the presence of something inexplicable and utterly beyond our ken. This "something" is what Otto calls the *mysterium tremendum*, the overwhelming mystery of existence.

While the inscrutable has a certain fascination for us, it can also be disquieting. We fill the void of the unknown with shapes of our own nightmarish imagining. And superstition is therefore closely related to religion. While one operates at an unconscious level and the other more consciously, both are the mind's response to a world that surpasses comprehension.

Fear of the supernatural, says Otto, is a universal feature of the human psyche. Every culture seems to populate the dark with its own horrific denizens: demons, genies, or poltergeists. While animals may or may not give such distinct form to their nocturnal forebodings, dread of the inexplicable seems to be an attribute we share with other species. And if it is true, as Otto claims, that this haunting feeling is the origin of the religious impulse, then human beings might not be the only spiritual creatures on this planet. My friend Elmer Fisk writes that not long after the dump episode his dog had another frightening experience:

> We had moved into our new home in Burlington, and Boob was sound asleep on the floor between the dining room table and the door to the patio. It was a blustery night in October, and the wind

was blowing the fallen leaves against the house. Suddenly a freak gust simultaneously blew open the storm door and inner door, and it noisily whisked through the opening a half bushel of dry oak leaves.

The leaves were aimed right at the spot where Boob was sleeping, but he was no longer there. With that first whoosh of the wind and rattle of leaves Boob sprang up a foot from the floor and landed running (running in place, until he got traction), all the while looking with bulging eyes back toward the door. Although it was an eerie couple of seconds, I didn't see anything come through the door except wind and leaves. But I think Boob thought the Devil came in, or that little green man from the dump.

In the substratum of the mind, animals and humans share memories of a time when the world was alive and magical, where the voices of departed ancestors mingle with the whispering leaves and blowing wind. And perhaps we share some sense of the preternatural, the uneasy suspicion that "there are more things in heaven and earth" than meet the eye or are revealed to the senses.

Do animals have a sense of the mysterious? They seem to. Like human beings, they inhabit a baffling world, and this may give rise to some rather unnerving fantasies. At the oddest times their fur bristles, they peer intently into empty space, or a guttural moan escapes their throats for no perceptible reason. Is it because they see a ghost or feel an invisible presence? Or because they sense, as we do, that the universe is an infinitely odd and enigmatic place?

No one can say for sure. But in the night all cats are black. And in the dark forests of the unconscious, all of us—beasts and humans—may look very much alike.

"All God's creatures have a place in the choir," runs a popular refrain. "Some sing lower, some sing higher, and some sing out from a telephone wire." But why do birds sing? Is it by instinct, or because of a creative impulse they share with human composers and musicians? The more we study animals and their songs, the clearer it becomes that human beings are not the only virtuosos in the orchestration of life.

4

Hearts of Song
Why Do Birds Sing?

People in our congregation love music. While I would like to believe that most of the worshipers come to hear my scintillating sermons, part of me knows it's not true. With a hundred-thousand-dollar organ and a forty-voice choir, we produce some truly amazing sounds on Sunday morning. Even at my most eloquent, I know that I'm no match for Handel or Vaughn Williams.

Human beings are not the only animals that appear to appreciate fine music. In the last century, an English musician named John Lockman visited a friend in the countryside, in Cheshire, where the family's daughter frequently played the piano. Whenever she played the air "Speri si" from Handel's opera, *Admetus,* a pigeon would descend from a dovecote adjacent to the window of the room where the girl sat "and listen to the air apparently with the most pleasing emotions," returning to its perch when the song was over. But it was only the "Speri si" that evoked such fascination from the opera-loving bird.[1]

Other species may have similar tastes. Noticing how her cat liked to sprawl across the top of the piano every time she sat down to practice, one music therapist decided to find out how other creatures might respond to such rhapsodies. She decided to conduct an experiment at a small dairy farm in Sidney, Indiana, where forty-two Holsteins who had never been exposed to music were treated to measured doses of Classical, Hard Rock, and Country & Western over a thirteen-day period. The results suggested that cows are a sophisticated audience. Milk production rose almost six percent when classical music was being aired (Beethoven's *Symphony No. 5 in C Minor* and Haydn's *Symphony No. 7 in C Major*) but fell by the same amount when the stereo played the rock band Kiss. Do all cows have such highbrow preferences? "As with humans, personalities vary in cows," the musical researcher concluded, noting that some bovines might adore Bach while others like to boogie.[2]

Who knows how many other animals are music lovers? The Greek historian Herodotus (c. 484−c. 425 B.C.E.) relates the tale of Arion, renowned in his day for his skill upon the harp. Returning by sea to his home in Corinth, Arion was accosted by the mutinous crew, who demanded his money and were prepared to throw him into the sea. Arion, as a last request, asked to play his instrument one final time upon the quarter-deck. When his tune was finished, he dove into the waves and was rescued by a dolphin, who had been attracted by the melody. The dolphin carried Arion safely back to shore. The story may be legendary but seems plausible. Dolphins and similar marine mammals are known for their complex acoustical compositions, and the white whale or Beluga has even been called "the canary of the sea." Yet when we think of creatures with a song in their hearts, the animals that immediately come to mind are not cats or cows or even cetaceans, but birds.

Birds, whom the composer Dvořák called "the true masters," are natural musicians. For centuries people wondered why birds sing and ascribed their melodies to "the glory of God." It was not until 1920, when Eliot Howard published his book, *Territory in Bird Life*, that a more rigorous theory of bird song began to emerge, as it became evident that birds sing for utilitarian reasons: to attract mates and to defend areas for nesting.

We now realize that in many avian species the most energetic singing is from males who have territories but lack partners. Faced with two suitors, a female will most likely bestow her favors on the one who sings more persistently. But the fact that such serenades have a sexual function does not necessarily mean they lack other levels of significance. A human flirtation helps propagate the species, too, but for the participants, it can also be a highly artful and enjoyable encounter.

I began to take an interest in birds several years ago. Each morning I walked to a small park near my home, where I would sit in meditation to start the day. After a few minutes of "watching the breath," I began to pay attention to my immediate surroundings. I especially noticed the gossip and chattering in the nearby brush. There were barn swallows, black-capped chickadees, and dark-eyed juncos there, but I had never heard them before. Birds and their music occupied a very small niche in my mental landscape. As they emerged into my awareness, though, I started to wonder about these feathered songsters. I became curious. Why do birds sing?

Perhaps it's true, as Gerard Manley Hopkins, the poet, suggests, that singing is the way a bird proclaims its own existence: "myself it speaks and spells, Crying *What I do is me: for that I came.*" A distinctive song helps the bird announce its presence, warding off potential interlopers and attracting females of the same species. But analysis shows most bird song to be much more complex than a simple cry of self-assertion.

Young birds begin to sing in much the way infants begin to speak: in a free-flowing, meandering exploration of sound. More than most other creatures birds have been shown to "play" with sounds—not only the sounds of their own voices but those that can be produced by manipulating their environment. Researchers have reported many instances of songbirds picking up and dropping objects, then repeating such performances over and over, apparently for the sheer pleasure of listening to the world chime and rattle.[3] Out of their childlike cooing and improvised chirping, maturing birds gradually build up their repertoire of more stereotyped (and functional) love songs.

It follows that most bird song involves a strong element of learning. Call notes and alarm cries appear to be innate, and it seems likely that when learning to sing most birds have an inborn preference for the sound patterns of their own species. In some species the song itself may be genetically coded. Yet listeners have documented numerous cases in which birds reared in captivity, isolated from adults of their own kind, have learned the "wrong" song. A Western Meadowlark, for instance, can sing like a Baltimore Oriole.[4]

Members of the same species, moreover, may develop differing "dialects" depending upon where they live—further evidence that singing is an acquired art. And highly imitative birds like the mockingbird and lyrebird of Australia can learn and duplicate the songs of many other species. A mockingbird may learn up to two hundred different songs, and lyrebirds have been known to reproduce the sounds of train whistles, automobile horns, and barking dogs as well as the melodies of their neighbors Down Under.

Bird song is therefore far from a mechanical performance. Just as the human brain may be "wired" for language but not wired to speak English, French, or Hindi, birds may be programmed for music without being locked into any one chorale. Crickets may hum and cicadas buzz more or less by instinct (although even insects can vary the frequency of their calls to synchronize their chorus), but birds have a high degree of freedom to choose what they sing.

Is it merely an accident that they choose to sing so beautifully? Not all birds are sonorous, of course. Of one bird, the Malabar Whistling Thrush, an ornithologist said that it "has forgotten its tune, but it whistles on," and most species use more harsh and discordant notes than even the most avant-garde human composers.[5] Suprisingly, many birds are relatively insensitive to pitch. But the best singers employ all the elements of tone, interval, rhythm, theme, and variation in complex and highly pleasing combinations. And what is music if not the deliberate arrangement of sound in aesthetic patterns?

When I asked the choir director at our church if bird song could be regarded as true music, he was strongly resistant to the idea. Only human compositions, in his opinion, are genuinely creative. Yet nothing in the nature of music excludes the music of nature. Birds cannot explain where their melodies come from, of course, but ultimately neither could Mozart. In a letter to a friend the great composer confessed that tunes simply floated into his head: *"Whence* and *how* they come, I know not; nor can I force them."

Music is an expression of our spiritual nature, welling up from inward springs and freshets. The composer Roger Sessions writes that music "reproduces for us the intimate essence, the tempo and the energy, of our spiritual being; our tranquillity and our restlessness, our animation and our discouragement, our vitality and our weakness—all, in fact, of the fine shades of dynamic variation of our inner life."[6] Music is the language of the soul.

The tempo of life is faster-paced for birds than for people. This is one of the reasons the individual notes in bird song are so short, sometimes distinguishable only with a spectrograph, and why the compositions of birds last a few seconds at most, compared to an hour or more for a human symphony. It is also why birds sing in the upper registers (just as the pitch on a phonograph record rises when played at high speed). To the birds, with a metabolism continually in allegro, human beings must appear to be lazy and dim-brained creatures indeed. Just as our music reflects the rhythm and intensity of our inner life, the music of birds expresses the flash and flutter of their nervous and high-strung existence.

But we may soon lose the pleasure of listening to their music. Recent counts show that the population of songbirds has plummeted. Whether because of pesticides or loss of habitat, the number of many species has declined as much as a third. Richard Coles, a biology professor at Washington University, has observed a thirty percent decline since 1980 in the number of migrating warblers—one of the more common songbirds, with about fifty species in North America—at the 2,000-acre Tyson Research Center wildlife refuge near St. Louis. Flocks of flycatchers, thrushes, vireos, and other singers are also disappearing. Some species, like cardinals, seem to be holding their own. But those that winter in the tropics have been especially hard-hit, and even those who reside year-round in northern climes have been affected by forest fragmentation, leaving them more susceptible to parasites and predation. With each passing year and each acre of land cleared for new homes and shopping malls, Rachel Carson's warning of a "silent spring" is coming closer to reality. Most of us probably don't notice the difference, but it is a slightly less musical world, a bleaker and more discordant world, as the noise of bulldozers drowns out the tunes of field and woodland.

It is also a less enchanting world. From ancient times birds have been associated in art, myth, and literature with the mystical domain of the spirit. For early Christians the Holy Ghost was pictured as a dove. In the *Mundaka Upanishad* of India the finite and the Supreme spirit (the lower self and the higher self) are likened to two birds clinging to one tree, the body. For the Greeks and Egyptians the ascent of the soul after death was represented by the upward flight of the *ba*, or soul-bird, and in Islamic art, the spirits of the departed flutter, birdlike, in paradise. It is no accident that angels are depicted with wings. Their freedom, their joy, their energy and vivacity have made birds natural symbols of the divine.

Birds inspire and uplift us with their carols. George Meredith, a novelist and poet of the nineteenth century, was the author of an anthem called "The Lark Ascending" that still appears in some church hymn books:

> In singing till his heaven fills,
> 'Tis love of earth the lark instills,
> And ever winging up and up,
> Our valley is his golden cup,
> And he the wine which overflows
> To lift us with him as he goes.

No, birds do not sing "for the glory of God." But they do share with us a creative impulse, and creativity is a hallmark of the Creator. For in every creative work there is an element that is transpersonal. In the music of both birds and humans, beauty is "the wine which overflows."

When the last lark has fallen silent, something holy will have vanished from the world. The chorus of life will be muted. The cathedral of the earth will have lost its choir.

NOTES

1. George J. Romanes, *Animal Intelligence* (New York: Appleton, New York, 1884), p. 282.
2. Alicia Evans, *Hoard's Dairyman*, September 10, 1990.
3. Charles Hartshorne, *Born to Sing* (Bloomington, IN: Indiana University Press, 1973), p. 51.
4. *Ibid.*, p. 49.
5. *Ibid.*, p. 46.
6. Brewster Ghiselin, ed., *The Creative Process* (Berkeley, CA: University of California Press, 1952), p. 46.

The poet Longfellow declared, "Nature is a revelation of God; Art is a revelation of man." But do other species have an artistic side? Can they appreciate design and color, form and beauty? Human beings are not the only creatures who express their inner visions through art. Other species also appear to possess an aesthetic urge.

5

Art for Art's Sake
Why Do Animals Draw?

"Some who know me would say that the main focus of my art is about getting dirty, hitting stuff with hammers, and playing with power tools," joked a friend of mine who is a well-known local sculptor. But there was something more serious that impelled him to weld and mold in metal, he added. "It's about passing through resistance to reclaim a purer vision, seeing with the beginner's mind, being connected to a spiritual source, grabbing hold of those high voltage transmission lines of the deeper energies that create, sustain and empower our souls."

My friend's talk was part of a Sunday service on "Religion and the Arts," an annual event at our church in which I invite members of the congregation who may be sculptors, potters, or printmakers to reflect on the relation between spirituality and the artistic process. The connection between the two became clear to me several years ago when I first started painting. Although my grandfather was an artist, my mother paints, and my brother teaches art, I had always been considered the "non-artistic" member of the family, so it took some courage to begin. But I now believe all people are artistic. Each of us has an aesthetic impulse. There is a deep-down satisfaction that comes from filling a beckoning canvas with bright colors and eye-pleasing shapes, and I often spend hours absorbed in my watercolors and acrylics. As my friend says, art is a form of soul work.

Apparently, we are not the only species with artistic inclinations. In 1982 Jerome Witkin, a professor of art at Syracuse University and a respected authority on abstract expressionism, was invited to view a collection of drawings by a "mystery artist." The professor was busy at the time, preparing for a traveling exhibition. Nevertheless, he was sufficiently intrigued to accept the invitation.

"These drawings are very lyrical, very, very beautiful," the professor said when he saw the portfolio. "They are so positive and affirmative and tense, the energy is so compact and controlled, it's just incredible."

"This piece is so graceful, so delicate," he said of one drawing. "I can't get most of my students to fill a page like this."[1]

Only after he had finished his professional evaluation did Witkin learn the identity of the artist:

a fourteen-year-old, 8,400-pound Asian elephant named Siri who lived in Syracuse's Burnet Park Zoo. Siri's keeper, David Gucwa, had seen her tracing lines with sticks and stones in the dust of her cage. Against the wishes of the zoo's superintendent, who scoffed at the notion of an artistic elephant, Gucwa had given her pads of paper and charcoal, permitting her to express herself more freely.

Siri is talented, but not unique, for all elephants draw. Some zoos have started to capitalize on this fact. Pachyderm paintings often fetch good prices with the public—one major difference between their canvasses and mine. But elephants are not in it for the money. They draw with or without a promoter to sell their work. They are the only animals we know of who do so spontaneously and without training.

This is not to imply that other animals don't like to draw. During the 1950s Desmond Morris carried out research on the artistic ability of nonhuman primates, who, once given the proper equipment, became quite adept with pens and pigments. In *The Biology of Art* Morris described the work of twenty-three chimpanzees, two gorillas, three orangutans, and four capuchin monkeys. One of them, a chimp named Congo, produced more than four hundred drawings, inspiring some to call him the Picasso of the Great Apes.[2]

Although mostly smudges and scribbles, the patterns the primates produced were far from random.

They demonstrated a distinct feel for symmetry and balance. If a drawing was started on one side of a blank page, the chimpanzee began to draw on the opposite side, presumably in order to offset the design. When presented with an unfinished figure such as a ring of several dots with one dot missing, the animal invariably supplied the dot needed to complete the configuration. Congo began his work with straight lines cross-hatched on the paper but eventually progressed to making fan shapes and even complete circles. All of the apes worked with gusto; Congo could paint happily for up to an hour, entranced with his own creations. "Both man and the apes have an inherent need to express themselves aesthetically," Morris concluded.[3] In other animals, as in human beings, there appears to be a delight in "art for art's sake."

Primate researcher Roger Fouts carried out similar investigations, holding the world's first exhibition of "chimpressionistic" art in 1981. The four animals who contributed to the show each had highly individual styles, he notes. Washoe did bright, wildly-colored compositions that she gave titles like "Electric Hot Red" (all of the animals had been taught to communicate in sign and named their own paintings). Another chimp, named Moja, may be the first nonhuman to paint representationally. She consistently uses a circular shape to illustrate a "berry" and a radial form for the figure of a "flower," but birds are her favorite subject, depicted by a series of swooping lines that may suggest the curvature of flight. Most of the chimps are less realistic in their approach. In a gesture worthy of a modern performance artist, Dar is known to eat his own paint, quite unlike his older sister Tatu, who becomes so engrossed in her work that she will frequently skip dinner rather than leave a painting unfinished. These animals obviously enjoy their dabbling. But does their work qualify as art?

Without directly answering that question, Fouts tells of a chimp named Ally he worked with during the 1950s whose highly energetic style bore a surprising resemblance to the "action painting" of Jackson Pollack, whose splattered canvasses were all the rage among the *cognoscenti* at that time. The similarity in techniques was ironic, since there were frequent comments from the man-in-the-street that a monkey throwing paint at an easel could create artworks every bit as good as "Jack the Dripper." On a lark, Fouts says, one of his students decided to get a more professional appraisal of Ally's work by showing it to an art historian, telling him that it had been done by a talented friend. The art historian was ecstatic. "I knew Pollack was coming back!" he exulted. Fouts doesn't say how the man reacted when he learned that the painting had been done by an ape.[4]

In the case of Siri, it didn't bother Jerome Witkin at all to learn that the art he praised so highly had been

71

produced by an elephant. "I'm even more impressed," he said. "Our egos as human beings have prevented us for too long from watching for the possibility of artistic expression in other beings."[5]

Art arises from a spiritual longing that all people share: to make our mark on the world and to spend our life energy in a work that rises above the mundane, adding grace to existence. We respond to the light of the world around us by giving expression to our own inner light, and when the two are on the same wavelength, the world seems more brilliant and finely focused. Is it possible that Siri's creations are products of a similar yearning for self-expression? Do elephants and apes as well as humans have an aesthetic impulse? How do we know what goes on in the mind of an elephant, or if an elephant has a mind? And how do we even begin to address such perplexing issues?

It was questions like these that fascinated Alan Turing, one of the inventors of the modern computer and a pioneer in the field of artificial intelligence. The puzzle that Turing thought about most keenly was the question of whether a computer would some day be able to think. Could a machine have a mind? Turing asked these questions at a time when computer science was in its infancy, and even today no one supposes that anything like human intelligence has been produced with programs or microchips. The issue, though, is whether or not it is theoretically possible. Can the spiritual arise from a purely material basis? Could a machine create art, or puzzle about the meaning of existence, or enjoy a joke, or worry about the fact that its circuits will one day be obsolete?

These are the kinds of questions on which people can dogmatize endlessly, but instead of doing that, Turing tried to take a more practical approach. He invented a way to test for the presence or absence of soul.

Turing's invention has come to be called the Turing Test, or Imitation Game. The test requires two type-writers (and today we might add two computer terminals) in separate rooms, linked with a connection that permits people to send messages from one room to the next. The test is to determine who (or what) is at the other keyboard: a human being or a machine. If a machine can fool a human interviewer into believing that he or she is talking to another person, then the machine has passed the test, said Turing. If it responds like a human being, with all the individuality, complexity, and quirkiness of a human being, then for all intents and purposes the machine has the equivalent of a human mind.

Turing's Test has some relevance to the question of whether Siri's creations qualify as genuine art, for animals, at least since the time of the philosopher Descartes, have been looked upon as biological machines. They are considered not merely *non*-human but *sub*-human, programmed by instinct to react in rule-bound and predetermined ways. Only human beings, in the Cartesian view, possess consciousness, free will, or moral and aesthetic sensibilities.

At least by implication, Turing challenges these prejudices. Siri's creations may not be Rembrandts, but if they can fool the experts they are at least very good fakes. If her drawings give every appearance of being the genuine article, there is no logical reason to deny them the status of real art.

Hope Irvine, chair of the Department of Art Education at Syracuse University and an authority on children's art, was also shown Siri's drawings without knowing the identity of the artist.

"These don't look to me like kids' drawings," she said. They appeared to her too accomplished to be the work of children, showing an unusual sensitivity to the thickness and directionality of line. "On the other hand, an adult could just dash off a drawing like this— yet these don't look dashed off, somehow, to me. I have the feeling that the drawings were not done in a vacuum, that there was an object in the person's mind, that it was relating to something—whether it was relating to music, or relating to movement, I don't know." Professor Irvine's final conclusion: "These would be unusual for a kid. I would say an adult did them."[6]

While I enjoy painting, I am not an expert on art. To me, some of Siri's drawings look like meaningless scribbles; others appear to be very graceful, with a strong sense of graphic design. Many have the clean, sparse look I associate with Japanese calligraphy: bold, black brushstrokes that have a forceful, definitive impact on the paper. The marks do not appear to be planned or premeditated, yet some spontaneous intelligence seems to be guiding them. There are a few I wouldn't mind hanging on my living room wall.

Jerome Witkin, in later reflection on Siri's *oeuvre*, compared it favorably with the work of Willem de Kooning. "Anyone who has been trained in any way in the now-established tradition of abstract expressionism realizes that an unconscious 'handwriting' exists, exposing either 'false' or 'correct' marks," Witkin observed. "People admire the drawings of Willem de Kooning, one of the principal artists of the century, because his marks seem so totally correct and honest in their attack on the page. Well, a lot of the drawings in front of me now have an energy, a kind of joy of responding, much like the best of de Kooning's work. I wish Willem de Kooning could see these."[7]

So inspired, David Gucwa and James Ehmann decided to mail a packet of elephant art to the great painter himself. Eighty years old at that time, Willem de Kooning continued to paint and draw in his studio in East Hampton, New York. Just then he was preparing for a one-man exhibition to be displayed on two floors of the Whitney Museum in Manhattan. Thus came into being another response to the artistic "Turing

Test," with results suggesting that other species, at least elephants, have real gifts for artistic expression. Elaine de Kooning, Willem's wife and herself an excellent artist, replied that she and her husband were impressed by the drawings.

> We felt they had a kind of flair and decisiveness and originality. Needless to say, we were dumbfounded when we read that they were made by an elephant.

> Mr. de Kooning said, "'That's a damned talented elephant." We discussed the drawings for about half an hour afterwards, and have been showing them to artist friends, all of whom are equally amazed.

> The drawings do not have a random quality. They are not accidental. They have the same kind of rhythm and verve one sometimes observes in the little dance steps elephants perform in zoos and circuses. Mr. de Kooning and I are both interested in following the career of this elephant.[8]

Siri's creations have a freshness and charm that draw raves from her admirers. Whether or not her sketches qualify as real art may depend upon our predispositions. At one level, seeing is believing; those who have viewed Siri's work without preconceived notions about the species of the artist have hailed its fine quality. At another level, believing is seeing; those who believe elephants to be "dumb animals" will probably never see much merit in Siri's efforts.

Have we been too hasty in classifying the family of life into artistic and non-artistic members? Is *Homo sapiens* the only species whose spirit is kindled by beauty? Perhaps the light and color of the universe awaken something radiant within Siri, calling forth her own inner illuminations. Can we at least consider the possibility that elephants paint for the same reason we do, for pure pleasure and enjoyment?

The great critic John Ruskin once said that art consists of "one soul talking to another." For those with eyes to see, Siri is an elephant with something meaningful to communicate.

NOTES
1. David Gucwa and James Ehmann, *To Whom It May Concern: An Investigation of the Art of Elephants* (New York: Norton, 1985), p. 4.
2. E.O. Wilson, *Sociobiology* (Cambridge, MA: Harvard University Press, 1980), pp. 288-289.
3. Desmond Morris, *The Biology of Art* (New York: Knopf, 1962), p. 151.
4. Roger Fouts with Stephen Tukel Mills, *Next of Kin: What Chimpanzees Have Taught Me About Who We Are* (William Morrow & Company, 1997), p. 161.
5. Gucwa, *op. cit.*, p. 6.
6. *Ibid.*, p. 106.
7. *Ibid.*, p. 119.
8. *Ibid.*, p. 120.

"Two things," wrote Immanuel Kant, "fill the mind with awe: the starry heavens above, and the moral sense within." But are human beings the only animals that have a moral sense or conscience? Do other creatures have notions of right and wrong? We are certainly not the only beings motivated by feelings of compassion and concern for others. Altruism is widespread in the animal world.

6

Evolutionary Ethics
Do Animals Know Right from Wrong?

Like most congregations, ours has a committed corps of people who come to the rescue when others are in need: visiting the sick, calling on the homebound, and staying in touch with those confined to nursing homes. In some churches, these good samaritans are known as the "caring committee." We call our resident angels the "lay ministry." I gained a firsthand appreciation of their work when, just as I was beginning to write this book, my wife and I both contracted pneumonia. Members of our congregation brought soup, casseroles, and vegetarian chili to our home to help our family through the illness, and they sent cards (decorated with elephants!) to boost our morale.

Caring for one another when we're sick is one of the ways we reach out in our church. A lot happens spontaneously. Someone needs a ride to the doctor, and somebody else volunteers to drive. No one seems to organize these efforts or think much about such everyday acts of charity. They are simply a natural expression of our concern for one another's well-being.

Animals seem to be endowed with the same generous impulses. One day my local newspaper carried a story about a young bottlenose dolphin in "a severely weakened state" that had appeared inside the surf line of Santa Monica Bay. Marine conservationists were uncertain about the precise nature of the animal's ailment. But six other adult dolphins had surrounded the sick mammal in an effort to keep it from beaching itself. Like people, dolphins care for their friends and family members who are ill.

Aristotle noticed this fact ages ago. "The story goes," he writes in his *History of Animals*, "that after a dolphin had been caught and wounded off the coast of Caria, a shoal of dolphins came into the harbor and stopped there until the fisherman let his captive go free; whereupon the shoal departed." Young dolphins are almost always followed by larger ones for protection, he observed.

Other creatures exhibit the same protective patterns. One of the other ministers on our staff, for instance, told me about a cedar waxwing that accidentally bumped into her picture window. Evidently, the birds had been feasting on the fermented berries in her backyard and become intoxicated. (Human beings are not the only creatures that revel in the happy hour, but other species have not yet invented the designated driver.) Fortunately, the bird was only stunned by the collision and dropped onto the dense foliage just below the pane of glass. As it lay motionless, two of its companions landed nearby, never departing more than a couple of feet from its side—very much like an avian caring committee. After an hour, the stricken bird had recovered sufficiently to fly once more. Together, the three birds took wing back into the trees.

Altruism is well-documented in the animal world. Chimpanzees in the wild lead hungry companions to trees with ripened fruit. Mother birds act as living decoys to lure predators away from the nests that contain their young. African wild dogs will attack a cheetah at great risk to their own lives in order to save a pup. Caring and sharing seem to "come naturally" to many species.

The first to make a systematic study of such behavior in animals was Charles Darwin in his book *The Descent of Man*. His conclusion was that "the difference in mind between man and the higher animals, great as it is, certainly is one of degree and not of kind."[1] Darwin pointed out that all social animals are endowed with feelings and impulses that tend to preserve the well-being of the group. Birds and mammals that flock or live in troops give alarm cries at the sign of danger, and some, like geese and seals, even post sentinels. This involves considerable self-sacrifice, for the one "on duty" puts itself at greater risk and forgoes opportunities for feeding and relaxation for the sake of its companions.

Animals also cooperate for the common defense, like sparrows that mob a hawk, or like a band of monkeys cited by Darwin. He saw an eagle seize a young monkey, who avoided being carried off by clinging to a branch. "It cried loudly for assistance," he wrote, "upon which the other members of the troop, with much uproar, rushed to the rescue, surrounded the eagle, and pulled out so many feathers that he no longer thought of his prey, but only how to escape."[2]

Pelicans and crows have been known to feed and care for blind comrades, and such cases, the great naturalist points out, must be far too rare to be chalked up to instinct. Clearly, animals can sympathize with others in distress.

Dogs have lived among people for so long that they often appear to have acquired human characteristics. Most canines respond readily to praise or blame and quickly internalize their master's expectations for good and bad behavior. My own dog Chinook, I recall, showed real remorse whenever I scolded him for digging in the flower beds. His whole expression changed: eyes averted, head downcast, hindquarters hung low. The reassurance that he was a good dog would instantly set his tail wagging again. Our new puppy, on the other hand, is not quite so sensitive to human approval. If I reprimand him, his repentance is heartfelt and sincere, albeit short-lived.

Like most dog lovers Darwin was convinced that "man's best friend" possesses something closely resembling a conscience. "There can, I think, be no doubt that a dog feels shame, as distinct from fear, and something very like modesty when begging too often for food. A great dog scorns the snarling of a little dog, and this may be called magnanimity," he states.[3]

Still, Darwin hesitated to say that animals possess a true ethical sense. Genuine morality, he felt, requires intellectual reflection and discrimination, comparing one's own actions against a universal moral code. He found no evidence that other animals possessed this capacity. "Therefore, when a Newfoundland dog drags a child out of the water, or a monkey faces danger to rescue its comrade, or takes charge of an orphan monkey, we do not call its conduct moral," he concluded.[4]

But what is morality? Is it primarily a question of reasoning about abstract principles? Or is it rather a matter of responding to the natural impulse to help another in need? Presumably, people were caring and considerate of one another long before they developed complicated moral philosophies. Aren't the people of simple, pre-literate societies just as moral as those who have studied ethics in libraries and universities?

Darwin was a magnificent biologist but a poor ethicist. He believed not only that animals lacked a moral sense but that "primitives" and "savages" were also deficient in this regard. Like most Victorian gentlemen he was convinced of the preeminent mental powers of educated Europeans, whom he believed to be intellectually as well as ethically superior to "less civilized" races. In Darwin's view, the powers of reasoning and moral reflection ascended slowly from brute creation to the drawing rooms and salons of polite society.

The morality of "savages," Darwin felt, was narrow and self-interested. Primitive people cared only for their own immediate clan or tribe; but gradually, in the course of moral evolution, human beings learned to expand their ethical vision beyond their own family and kin groups to wider and more inclusive perspectives. "As man advances in civilization," Darwin wrote, "and small tribes are united into larger communities, the simplest reason would tell each individual that he ought to extend his social instincts and sympathies to all the members of the same nation, though personally unknown to him. This point being once reached, there is only an artificial barrier to prevent his sympathies extending to the men of all nations and races."[5] What Darwin failed to see is that the barrier between people and animals is equally artificial.

The word "kin" is cognate with the word "kind." This connection suggests that we are most sensitive to the needs and feelings of those we recognize as "our own flesh and blood." Beings whom we feel to be fundamentally like ourselves receive our solicitous attention while those whom we see as alien are excluded from the circle of our care. The question is: what are the ethically relevant characteristics that qualify another being as a member of our moral community?

At various times, race, skin color, and other superficial qualities have been used to deny the rights of others and exclude them from our affection and concern. And just as nineteenth-century Europeans justified colonialism with the rationalization that "primitives" and "savages" were mentally and morally inferior, we continue to justify exploitation of the animal world in the same way. By denying that animals possess a moral sense we tell ourselves that human beings are of a fundamentally higher order. We can therefore colonize and enslave with impunity those who are "lower."

It is important to recognize that Darwin himself never drew such conclusions from his theory. He was a lifelong opponent of slavery and engaged in bitter feuds on the subject with Robert Fitzhugh, the captain of the HMS *Beagle,* during their long voyage of discovery. He also condemned any form of cruelty to animals. The memory of human chattel being mistreated in Brazil troubled him for years, according to his son, who also recalled his father on at least one occasion returning from his daily walk pale and shaken from having seen a horse being abused by its owner. Darwin was made faint from the agitation of having violently remonstrated with the man. The thought of any creature in pain was almost unbearable, and in a letter to Professor Ray Lankester, the eminent biologist confessed that the practice of experimentation on living beings made him "sick with horror." Darwin mused, "Every one has heard of the dog suffering under vivisection, who licked the hand of the operator; this man, unless the operation was fully justified by an increase of our knowledge, or unless he had a heart of stone, must have felt remorse to the last hour of his life." While animal research might be a terrible necessity in some circumstances, he felt, it should never be pursued for "mere damnable and detestable curiosity." With a better understanding than most others of how closely we are all related, the great scientist was also a great humanitarian.

Yet even Darwin, who taught that we are all descendants of a common ancestor, was reluctant to grant animals a moral sense comparable to our own. For conscience, traditionally, has been considered the seat of the soul. The knowledge of good and evil, and the power to choose between them, is thought to be an essential part of what makes us as human. But how would our attitude toward other species change if we believed them to be our moral as well as biological kin, capable of benevolence, courage, and other "human" virtues? An answer may come from Darwin's contemporary and colleague, the ethologist George

Romanes, who relates the following incredible account of animal herosim.

Romanes says that a friend of his, a naturalist collecting specimens of bird life, shot a tern, which fell wounded into the sea. The bird's companions hovered about, "manifesting much apparent solicitude, as terns and gulls always do under such circumstances." Attended by its friends, the wounded bird began drifting shorewards, and the hunter made ready to collect his trophy. But to his "utter astonishment and surprise," he saw two of the unwounded terns "take hold of their disabled comrade, one at each wing, lift him out of the water, and bear him seawards." They were followed by two other birds. After the wounded bird had been carried about six or seven yards, he was set gently down again, "when he was taken up in a similar manner by the two who had been hitherto inactive. In this way they continued to carry him alternately, until they had conveyed him to a rock at a considerable distance, upon which they landed him in safety."

Recovering his composure, the hunter once again prepared to retrieve the wounded tern. As the other birds observed him, however, the whole swarm descended, as if to block his path. And before he could claim his prize, the bird was again rescued by the others.

On my near approach to the rock I once more beheld two of them take hold of the wounded bird as they had done already, and bear him out to sea in triumph, far beyond my reach. This, had I been so inclined, I could no doubt have prevented. Under the circumstances, however, my feelings would not permit me; and I willingly allowed them to perform an act of mercy which man himself need not be ashamed to imitate.[6]

One "good tern" deserves another. And if teamwork, cooperation, self-sacrifice, and bravery under fire are considered moral virtues, these birds displayed all the marks of morality. How can we even think of shooting such creatures? Animals of such daring and compassion should not be used for target practice.

In the long course of our moral and spiritual evolution, says Darwin, we have gradually learned to broaden the circle of our concern for others. Perhaps it is time now to bring not only other races and nations but other species within that arc. "Sympathy beyond the confines of man," he notes, "that is, humanity to the lower animals, seems to be one of the latest moral acquisitions."[7] But we must realize that other animals are not lower than ourselves, only different.

While their loyalties are different from our own, animals still have loyalties. While their sympathies are strange to us, they still have sympathies. Not all animals are social, of course, and only a few are altruistic. Not all animals (and not all people) have moral capacities or know right from wrong. But almost all suffer like us and bleed when wounded. Under the skin, be it smooth, furred, or feathered, we are all related.

We are kin to, and must be kind to, all creation. Overcoming speciesism—the illusion of human superiority—will be the next step in our moral and spiritual evolution.

NOTES
1. Charles Darwin, *The Descent of Man* (New York: A.L. Burt, 1874), p. 148.
2. *Ibid.*, p. 115.
3. *Ibid.*, p. 74.
4. *Ibid.*, p. 126.
5. *Ibid.*, p. 139.
6. Romanes, *op. cit.*, p. 275.
7. Darwin, *op. cit.*, p. 139.

"What greater thing is there for two human souls," asked George Eliot, *"than to feel that they are joined for life?"* Do animals also experience love? Do they know the meaning of devotion and fidelity to their mates? Love is the noblest expression of our humanity; it is also one of the bonds that links us with other living creatures. Love is a form of symbiosis: the joining of separate organisms in the service of a greater life. Human or otherwise, those who abide in love abide in God, and God abides in them.

7

Partners for Life
Do Animals Experience Love?

Whether the ceremony consists of two people exchanging rings in the privacy of their living room or a gala affair with bridesmaids, ringbearers, and yards of white satin, a wedding is always a momentous occasion. The decision to marry is one of the most important we ever make, for it is intended to last a lifetime. Each time I perform a wedding, I am conscious of the solemnity of this commitment, and I try to find words that express its significance. I often read from Paul's first letter to the Corinthians, which contains one of the great tributes to human love:

> Love is patient and kind; love is not jealous or boastful; it is not arrogant or rude. Love does not insist on its own way; it is not irritable or resentful; it does not rejoice at wrong, but rejoices in the right. Love bears all things, believes all things, hopes all things, endures all things.

I find this passage especially appropriate for weddings. While physical attraction may draw a couple together, for the relationship to endure other qualities are needed: constancy, patience, flexibility, and persistence.

Many unions last for years, but the lustre fades. Warm and tender feelings may give way to cool indifference. The fascination of romance yields to the dullness of daily routine. Our soaring divorce rate suggests that the pledge to love "for better or worse, for richer or poorer, in sickness and in health" expresses an ideal few partners actually attain.

Not so among the jackdaws. Like wild geese, jackdaws are one of the species of birds that mate for life. Konrad Lorenz, in his book *King Solomon's Ring*, compares their love lives favorably with those of their human counterparts.

In outward appearance jackdaws resemble their relatives the crows. They are long-lived creatures, and their unions outlast many a human marriage. "But even after many years," says Lorenz, "the male still feeds his wife with the same solicitous care, and finds for her the same low tones of love, tremulous with inward emotion, that he whispered in his first spring of betrothal and of life."[1]

Like human beings jackdaws "fall in love" in head-over-heels fashion. Somewhat inexplicably, romance simply blossoms. "And in this connection, many higher birds and mammals behave in exactly the same way as the human being," affirms Lorenz. "Very often even in jackdaws the 'Grand Amour' is quite suddenly there, from one day to the next—indeed most typically, just as in the case of man, at the moment of the first encounter."[2]

While jackdaws may be smitten with "love at first sight," they tend to be old-fashioned birds, and there is no hasty retreat to the bedroom. Like many avian species, they have a lengthy period of engagement. Among jackdaws, there is usually a full year of courtship between the "betrothal," when pair-bonds are formed, and the "wedding," when the relationship is consummated.

"The betrothed pair form a heart-felt mutual defense league, each of the partners supporting the other most loyally," says Lorenz.

This militant love is fascinating to behold. Constantly in an attitude of maximum self-display, and hardly ever separated by more than a yard, the two make their way through life. They seem tremendously proud of each other, as they pace ponderously side by side. . . . And it is really touching to see how affectionate these two wild creatures are with each other. Every delicacy that the male finds is given to his bride and she accepts it with the plaintive begging gestures and notes otherwise typical of baby birds. In fact, the love-whispers of the couple consist chiefly of infantile sounds, reserved by adult jackdaws for these occasions. Again, how strangely human![3]

Some sophisticates may think it sentimental to ascribe such refined feelings as love to a pair of nesting birds. But Lorenz counters that love is widespread throughout the animal kingdom. It is, in fact, an age-old impulse. Love is, after all, concerned less with the head than with the heart. And while the enlargement of the neocortex is a fairly recent evolutionary phenomenon, the growth of the limbic system (the gray matter that surrounds the brain stem and that governs the emotions) began long ago. These regions of the brain are quite well-developed among birds. While there may be an intellectual gulf between human beings and jackdaws, the emotional gulf may be slight.

Birds appear to have whatever neural equipment they need to experience infatuation, jealousy, and all the other pangs of the lovelorn. When one of the birds Lorenz studied lost its mate—the bird was eaten by a fox—the survivor subsequently showed all the signs of grief: listlessness, loss of appetite, drooping head, and downcast eyes. "In terms of emotions," says Lorenz, "animals are much more akin to us than is generally assumed."[4] To call the mating behavior of jackdaws "love" is not a case of projecting human characteristics onto animals, therefore, but of recognizing animal characteristics in human beings.

It should not surprise us, then, to find that the love lives of other species compare advantageously with our own. Geese, like jackdaws, are also famous for their fidelity to their partners. Once the intially shy female has warmed up to the romantic posturing of the gander and joined him in the "triumph-call," the two are wed for life.

One morning many years ago, a farmer living near Buenos Aires witnessed the heart-rending tenacity of this love when he went riding on horseback and noticed on the plain ahead of him two geese, a white male and a brown female, walking in the distance. Drawing closer, he observed that the female was plodding steadily southward. The male, greatly agitated, walked about forty or fifty yards ahead of her, periodically rising into the air with forlorn cries. After flying a short way the gander turned back to rejoin his mate in her weary march. This pattern was repeated again and again. The female had broken her wing and, unable to fly, had set forth afoot on her fall migration to the Magellanic Islands. Driven by his deepest instincts to fly south, the male nevertheless refused to abandon his partner, but remained loyal in her hour of need, plaintively begging her to spread her wings and join him in the long flight home. The pair was truly faithful "until death do us part."[5]

Jackdaws and geese are exceptional creatures, of course. Only a few other birds—swans, ravens, and some eagles—mate for life. Most have love lives as confused and awkward as our own. Some birds have trouble finding a mate of the right species (sparrows look pretty much alike, for instance, not only to bird watchers but to others sparrows as well—thus the importance of a distinctive song in locating a proper partner). When the female and male wear similar plumage, birds may have difficulty telling boy from girl; grebes are notoriously puzzled about what sex they are, and the female mounts the male more often than not. The mating game is no less complicated for other species than it is for our own.

Nor is lovemaking among birds always sweet and gentle. Several years ago, while working as a volunteer in a wildlife clinic, I helped care for a female duck that had been "raped" by a gang of males. If some birds are models of marital devotion, others are far more casual in their relationships. But we need not idealize animals to observe that a powerful force of nature draws two creatures together, in spite of all the problems and perils involved, and to recognize something wonderful in this attraction.

This is my sense of it, anyway. Whenever I officiate at a wedding, solemnizing the bond of affection between two human souls, I feel that I am in the presence of a sacrament as old as the hills. When two lovers meet at the altar to become husband and wife, they are engaging in a ritual that has been repeated almost since the world began. Matrimony, according to *The Book of Common Prayer*, is "an estate instituted by God and made honorable by the faithful keeping of good women and men in all ages," but it predates humankind by millions of years. Love is so deep it is rooted in our very biology.

Through love we are joined with what is deepest in ourselves, and in the most intimate part of our lives we discover what is most universal. "Love," says the theologian Paul Tillich, "is life itself in its actual unity." We witness and celebrate that unity in marriage. Through the interwoven mysteries of sex, love, and procreation, life perpetuates itself and evolves. The earth maintains its vitality, and the universe is renewed.

Love is the desire in every beating heart to be joined with a larger and more lasting life. Is love a human quality? Is it animal? Some say it is divine. So faith, hope, and love abide, these three; but the greatest of these is love.

NOTES
1. Konrad Lorenz, *King Solomon's Ring* (New York: Crowell, 1952), p. 159.
2. *Ibid.,* p. 153.
3. *Ibid.,* p. 158.
4. Konrad Lorenz, *The Year of the Greylag Goose* (New York: Harcourt Brace Jovanovich, 1978), p. 31.
5. W.H. Hudson, *Birds and Man* (New York: Knopf, 1923), pp. 183-184.

Anyone who has ever teased a puppy with a sock or tantalized a kitten with a ball of yarn knows that animals love to play. Ponies prance, lambs frisk, and otters are born comedians. But why do creatures play? What purpose does play serve? The difficulty in finding a purpose in such cavorting may be related to the difficulty of finding a single purpose in life. Play, for humans as well as animals, exists for the sheer exuberance of being.

8

The Play's the Thing

Why Do Whooping Cranes Dance?

All the earth kicks up its heels in the springtime. Things start hopping—animals included. More than two thousand years ago, the philosopher Plato noticed how creatures like to leap. The natural motion of the soul is upward, the ancient Greeks speculated, which might explain why so many species have a propensity to propel themselves straight off the ground. Dolphins and orcas skyrocket out of the surf. Kangaroo rats bound high in the moonlight. Even hippos have been recorded doing the occasional back somersault.[1] People also get a little giddy when the weather warms up. In the first church I served, we danced the May Pole each year to celebrate nature's rebirth.

While our style of dancing, with children winding colored streamers around the pole, is of recent vintage, May Day itself is an ancient festival. In early times, the Druids of Old England believed the spirits of trees could bring new life at the season when the world was in bud and blossom. So trees were cut down in May and set in the village center while the townsfolk paraded about.

Later, Morris Men joined the festivities with their bright ribbons and bells. The bells jingled to help awaken the earth. The dancers leapt as high as they could, in hopes that the grain would grow equally high in the months to follow. Or men being men, the Morris Dancers may have just enjoyed showing off and displaying their prowess.

In any case, there's something about the end of winter that makes us want to jump for joy, and this appears to be just as true for other creatures as it is for human beings.

One of spring's most sprightly dancers is the whooping crane. A pair of cranes begins the dance, each spiralling about the other with wings half spread, taking quick, stiff steps and bowing deeply to the partner. One of the birds will suddenly leap straight into the air, catapulting as much as twenty feet off the ground. The other follows suit, and the two continue in a light-hearted acrobatic ballet. Poking and stabbing with their beaks, they toss bits of stick and straw into the air, catching them as they fall. It's an altogether unlikely sight and serves no discernible purpose. Nature, whom we like to think is lawful and majestic in her ways, is caught in a prankish and jesting mood.

I've never seen the dance myself—not surprising, since so few whooping cranes are left now. At one point early in this century there were only fifteen birds in the entire world. The first efforts to preserve the whooping crane began in 1937, when the birds' wintering area on the Texas Gulf Coast was designated an official refuge. It was evident that special efforts to breed them were needed if the cranes were to survive.

Zoos joined in the effort to save the endangered birds, but rearing cranes can be tricky. The San Antonio Zoo found that chicks seldom survived when left with their natural parents. So when an especially delicate hatchling named Tex peeped out of the shell one spring, the zoo's manager decided to rear her by hand. One unforeseen side effect of this unusual mother/child relationship, however, was that Tex imprinted on her human caregiver. As a result, she developed a lasting passion for the company of human beings instead of other whooping cranes.

That bit of confusion led to one of the strangest dances ever. When Tex reached the age of consent she was moved to the International Crane Foundation in Baraboo, Wisconsin, and supplied with a paramour named Tony, a male crane donated by the Audubon Park Zoo in New Orleans. But Tex and Tony represented the classic case of unrequited love. There was nothing lacking in Tony's ardor. The fault lay with Tex. The male's every overture was rejected. Because a female whooping crane ovulates in response to the proper courtship rituals from its mate, artificial insemination was out of the question, too. In cranes, as in *Homo sapiens*, the most powerful sex organ appears to be located in the brain, and this finicky bird clearly had an attitude problem. The crane had a crush on people, whom she considered to be her own species. But before she could be impregnated, Tex had to be brought into the rapture of romance.

It was amid this unhappy state of affairs that George Archibald, the director of the crane center, decided to take matters into his own hands. With the inspiration born of desperation, he prepared his gambit. If Tex wasn't excited by other cranes, George would do the courting himself.

In the spring of 1978 George and Tex literally shacked up together. George moved into a small wooden hut inside the whooper's pen. "Until then," George reported, "no one had spent any time with her since she was a chick. This was her first chance to make friends with a male of what she considered her species. I talked to her a lot, and she began to respond. I spent every spare moment with her. A pair bond formed."[2]

For two seasons George wooed the reluctant bird, not entirely without results. Twice, with the help of sperm donated by Tony and his brother Angus, Tex was successfully inseminated. One egg turned out to be infertile, though. The next year the chick in another egg died in the shell.

George decided to give it one last try. For six weeks in 1982 he camped out with the bird, taking on the role of devoted suitor. He helped Tex gather grasses for a nest. When Tex was tired, they rested together quietly. Most important, George danced, running and leaping, spinning and turning pirouettes, and spreading his arms like wings. To his delight, Tex joined in the dancing. At last Tex laid her long-awaited egg, and a month later a new whooping crane was born.

No one is quite sure why cranes dance, but perhaps it is for the same reason we dance the May Pole. It may simply be a manifestation of natural high spirits. Those who have seen the dance say it is unforgettable. The whooping crane is an enormous bird—a full-grown male may weigh twenty-five pounds and stand more than four feet tall with a seven-and-half-foot wingspan. To see this feathered giant and his mate capering like the Lord and Lady of the May is to witness one of the most extravagant rites of nature. The ritual is linked with courtship proceedings in the spring, but it goes on at other times of the year as well. In Japanese folklore the cranes are known for their *joie de vivre:* "the birds of happiness," they are called.

There is more here than can be explained by purely naturalistic causes. As Johan Huizinga points out in his book, *Homo Ludens: A Study of the Play Element in Culture,* play has a spiritual quality.[3] A world in which cranes dance has an element of carousing and freewheeling built into its very foundation. Animal scientists often try to explain play in terms of its survival value. Exploratory behavior like play, they point out, allows the organism to acquire information about its environment that may later prove useful. In hunting or fighting games a young animal can practice and perfect skills it will need in adulthood.

But while theories that explain play in terms of its later utility may be true in part, they are incomplete, says Huizinga. "As a rule they leave the primary quality of play, as such, virtually untouched. To each and every one of the above 'explanations' it might well be objected: 'So far so good, but what actually is the *fun* of playing?'"

It would be easy to imagine animals training for the demands of survival mechanically and mirthlessly, without sport or amusement. But while play may prepare us to cope with more serious business, play is itself not serious. It is carefree and teasing. And it is this "fun element" that characterizes play and that cannot be reduced to any other category.

This means that play has a psychic dimension. "In acknowledging play you acknowledge mind, for whatever else play is, it is not matter. Even in the animal world it bursts the bounds of the physically existent," says Huizinga. Animals play not because they have to but because they want to, and from this it follows that animals, like us, are the sorts of sophisticated beings who can be either bored or amused.

A creature who plays, moreover, is essentially unpredictable, full of tricks, feints, and surprises. "Animals play, so they must be more than merely mechanical things," states Huizinga. "We play and know that we play, so we must be more than merely rational beings, for play is irrational."

We live in a whimsical universe, one in which a spirit is "at play" behind the varied forms of creation. "Play cannot be denied," declares Huizinga. "You can deny, if you like, nearly all abstractions: justice, beauty, truth, goodness, mind, God. You can deny seriousness, but not play." Frolicking is everywhere, glad and irrepressible, confounding our desire for an orderly and logical world.

If you don't believe it, just watch a whooper in flight. "In fine, calm weather," an observer reported to *Forest and Stream* way back in 1883, the whooping crane "delights to mount up, in great, undulating spirals, to the height of a mile or so, and take a quiet float, while he whoops at neighbors in adjoining counties. After airing himself to his heart's content, he descends, sometimes spirally as he rose, at other times with great plunges and wild, reckless dives, until within about fifty feet of the earth when he hangs himself upon the air, with his long, spindling legs down, gently settles and alights." From the description, it's hard to say who is having more fun: the bird enjoying its flight or the person observing its antics.

Whooping cranes are slowly making a comeback. There are now about 250 birds living in the wild, including a new, non-migrating flock that was introduced to Florida in 1993, with another 125 cranes in captivity. Tex is no longer living, but her chick, named Gee Whiz, is alive and well. Gee Whiz is a cocky and somewhat aggressive fellow, and after an ill-fated affair with a bird named Faith, the matchmakers in Baraboo paired him with a demure young crane named Oobleck. Together the happy couple has produced eggs for each of the past two seasons. So the *pas de deux* continues.

Each of us participates in the dance of life. One great, gay spirit animates us all. And in the springtime, there is a skip in our step and a bounce in our walk. Cranes cavort and people promenade, probably for the same reason. We revel together in the rhythms of the earth. For life is ultimately a gambol—a leap of faith, a jump for joy, a mood of exultation shared by all created beings.

Shall we bow to our partners the animals? Shall we invite them to be our playmates? The May Pole is a merry reminder: all of us spring from a single Tree of Life.

NOTES
1. "Animals at Play," Stuart L. Brown, *National Geographic* (December, 1994), p. 30.
2. "Our Far-Flung Correspondents," Faith McNulty, *The New Yorker* (January 17, 1983), pp. 88-89.
3. Johan Huizinga, *Homo Ludens* (Boston, MA: Beacon, 1955), pp. 3-4.

It is difficult to probe the inward awareness of another being. The realm of what one mystic called "the interior castle" is wholly private and wrapped in solitude. But when we look into another's eyes—even into the eyes of an animal—we may find a small window into that inner sanctum, a window through which our souls can hail and greet one another.

9

The Eyes of Hope
Are Animals Conscious of Themselves?

A gifted and sensitive clergyman can read a great deal from another person's eyes. This was reconfirmed for me not long ago when I was asked to be part of a panel discussion for a high-school humanities class. First, a Catholic nun, a Jewish rabbi, and I each spoke briefly on the theme, "Where Do We Find Hope in Today's World?" Then, after twenty minutes, we opened the floor for discussion by inviting questions and comments from the class.

The audience of teenagers remained impassive and silent—a typical group of "sullen adolescents"—and the communication gap grew more and more uncomfortable. Finally, the rabbi looked at one of the boys seated at a desk about three rows back. "I can see a question in your eyes," the rabbi said. The boy blushed slightly and responded, "Yes, I do have a question," and then proceeded to ask about the rabbi's experiences as a military chaplain during World War II. From that point onward, the discussion flowed. I was amazed at the rabbi's perspicacity and his ability to intuit what the boy was thinking. The eyes are truly the windows of the soul.

Some people are more perceptive than others. I have never been good at reading people's eyes, for instance, but others are usually very good at reading mine. I'm an incompetent liar and not very good at feigning interest when I'm bored or distracted. Other people take one look at me and know immediately if I'm emotionally present or if my mind is elsewhere. The eyes sometimes speak more eloquently (and more truthfully) than words.

The act of making eye contact with another being presupposes a conscious self behind either pair of peepers: I see you seeing me, and I am aware that you are aware that we are looking at each other. Philosophers debate the problem of "other minds" and ask how we know that such minds exist, but I challenge such a philosopher to look me straight in the eye and tell me I'm a figment of his own imagination. We look into the eyes of politicians and salesmen to see if they're honest or deceitful. We peer into the eyes of lovers to see if their hearts are true. The eyes give clues to a person's character and inward condition.

A soulful gaze is the quickest route we have into another creature's awareness. There are many good reasons to believe that animals are conscious of themselves, as we are—that they not only experience the world, but reflect on that experience and have thoughts, cares, and worries as we do—but most of the evidence is indirect. The closest we come to actually touching the interior of another animal is through the eyes.

Just because I've never had a sense of making eye contact with a fish or a snake is no proof that these simpler creatures lack self-awareness. On the other hand, the fact that I have been able to establish eye contact with dogs, apes, and other mammals constitutes fairly good evidence (in a region where no evidence can be absolutely convincing) that these animals share with human beings a certain degree of self-consciousness.

Many people have had this experience of visual interplay with another animal. In *The Jungle Book*, Rudyard Kipling elaborates on the mystique of the eyes when he suggests that the human child, Mowgli, gains power over the the other creatures of the forest with his penetrating gaze. "If he stared hard at any wolf," says Kipling of Mowgli, "the wolf would be forced to drop his eyes." This is fiction, of course. In a recent book R.D. Lawrence turns Kipling on his head as he describes the real-life experience of looking into the eyes of an untamed wolf:

As we studied each other, I became aware that although he was prepared to be friendly, he was also still subjecting me to intense scrutiny. . . . Hypnotically impelling, Shawano's glowing eyes probed into my being, reading me, looking for weakness, for fear, for aggression—above all, for honesty. No one can deceive the eyes of a wolf.[1]

Although no words are spoken, we experience real communication when our eyes encounter those of another animal. Like those of a human being, such eyes can hold a range of emotions: reproach, remorse, defiance, or disdain. Those who work regularly with animals accept this as a matter of course. "For a long time I never liked to look a chimpanzee straight in the eye," says wildlife researcher Jane Goodall. "I assumed that, as is the case with most primates, this would be interpreted as a threat or at least as a breach of good manners. Not so. As long as one looks with gentleness, without arrogance, a chimpanzee will understand, and may even return the look." She continues:

Often I have gazed into a chimpanzee's eyes and wondered what was going on behind them. I used to look into Flo's, she so old, so wise. What did she remember of her younger days? David Greybeard had the most beautiful eyes of them all, large and lustrous, set wide apart.

They somehow expressed his whole personality,
his serene self-assurance, his inherent dignity—
and from time to time, his utter determination
to get his way.[2]

There is great reciprocity, a real fellow-feeling, that
comes from the exchange of glance. While the eyes do
not reveal fully, neither can they totally conceal the
presence of another conscious entity.

Looking into another person's eyes may enable us
to see that person in a softer and warmer light. In
her book, *Despair and Personal Power in the Nuclear Age,*
Joanna Rogers Macy offers a meditation, based on
the Buddhist practice known as the Brahmaviharas,
in which participants sit in pairs, peering into each
others' eyes.[3] As we engage in this exercise, we reflect
upon the gifts and strengths hidden within those
eyes, the resources of ingenuity and endurance as
well as the griefs and disappointments concealed
within their depths.

In using this exercise at workshops and worship
services I have found it very powerful. It can make people nervous at first. When our eyes meet, there is no
place to hide. We feel quite vulnerable and exposed, as
if our innermost soul is bared. For that very reason,
however, the exercise offers a chance to connect at a
profound and direct level—to establish a bond at the
very core of our being.

Macy relates that she used this exercise for the first time in Holland at a conference on world development. Among those present were a professor from Germany and a Dutch farmer who had fought the Nazis during the 1940s. Early in the conference the two had found themselves in heated conflict over a report given by the Chinese delegation, and they were no longer on speaking terms. But as luck would have it the two were paired off for Macy's meditation. "The next morning," she says, "I walked into the plenary session to find them sitting side by side, one's arm around the other's shoulders as they studied the day's agenda." The Dutchman told her that at first he and the German had glared at each other like boys in a staring contest. But when each was invited to contemplate the loneliness and anguish hidden behind the other's eyes, the wall of defiance crumbled. Anger, fear, and mistrust were replaced by the bond of shared humanity.

Where do we find hope in today's world? I find it in the ability of an elderly rabbi to catch the glimmer of curiosity in a young boy's eyes. I find hope in our ability to truly see and become conscious of each other. When we meet face-to-face and see eye-to-eye, we find that our differences of age, background, and even species are less important than the spirit that unites us.

There is an old Latin motto, *lupus est homo homini*, that means "man is a wolf to man." Finding peace within and bringing peace to the world may start with the capacity to look into another's eyes and to recognize there a kindred soul—whether the eyes belong to a German, a Dutchman, a friend or stranger, a chimpanzee, or even a wolf.

What do we see when we look into the eyes of another living creature? A lesser being? An object of indifference? Or can we look more deeply? Can we touch the inwardness of that animal and empathize with its joys and concerns? Can we see other animals as they are, different from us but not wholly unlike ourselves? Here is an interspecies meditation you might like to try:

Look into the eyes of an animal. It might be your dog or cat. Or, if you like, select one of the creatures whose photographs appear in this book. And as you look into those eyes, reflect that this being is a never-to-be-duplicated expression of the universe.

Pay attention to what you see: the years of living present within those eyes and the vitality that shines through their color and transparency.

Contemplate their shape. Notice the angles and curves of individuality that make the face of this creature a unique work of art, crafted by time and desire.

And as you look into this being's eyes, pay attention also to what you cannot see: the inwardness, the selfhood, the "I" that is as singular as its outward expression.

What you look upon is a living spirit. Greet and respect it. Appreciate it for what it is.

Ask yourself: What does it feel like to be this creature?

What does the world look like through its eyes?

Become aware of the great antiquity within those eyes—the millenia of evolution they hold within their gaze.

Sense a solitude you can never fully enter into or understand.

Be aware that this is a being who has known hardships and hurts you can never imagine. This is a being who has known moments of wildness and innocence that you can never share.

Yet this is a creature who is alive and has desires like you. It walks the same ground and breathes the same air. It feels pain and enjoys its senses—the dazzling warmth of the sun, the cooling shade of the forests, the refreshing taste of pure water—as you do. And in this we are all kin.

In that kinship, all life exists. Through that kinship we can find wholeness. Out of that kinship we can draw wisdom and understanding for the healing of our common home.

NOTES

1. R.D. Lawrence, *In Praise of Wolves* (New York: Holt, 1986), as quoted in *New York Times Book Review,* June 28, 1986.
2. Jane Goodall, *Through a Window: My Thirty Years with the Chimpanzees of Gombe* (Boston, MA: Houghton Mifflin, 1990), as quoted in *New York Times Book Review,* November 11, 1990.
3. Joanna Rogers Macy, *Despair and Personal Power in the Nuclear Age* (Philadelphia, PA: New Society, 1983), pp. 158-160.

"What is man without the beasts?"
asked Chief Seattle. "If all the beasts
were gone, men would die from a great
loneliness of spirit." How will human
beings be affected if animals vanish
from our world? Without our four-
legged and winged brothers and sisters
to share our lives, will we lose part of
our own souls? "Whatever happens to
the beasts soon happens to man," said
Chief Seattle. "All things are connected."

10

The Reflecting Self

Would We Lose Our Own Souls in a World without Animals?

One of the greatest privileges of my profession comes when I am asked to preside at the christening of a newborn baby. The little ones sometimes cry or wiggle, or they may even sleep through the entire ceremony, but that doesn't detract from the significance of the event. While I have welcomed hundred of infants into the world in this way, including two children of my own, I never cease to feel that I am in the presence of something extraordinary, on the boundary of what is utterly mundane and what is totally miraculous.

Millions of children are born each day, but each one is completely individual. Out of its mother's body, a tiny being, unprecedented and unique, emerges into the light. Where did it come from? How was it formed? What forces have conspired to create such a marvel? Knowing the facts of genetics and reproduction does little to lessen the wonderment. A brand new person has come into existence. A soul unlike any other has sprung into being.

How is it possible? Some religions teach that there is a distinct moment when a child is "ensouled," when the infant receives the crucial gift that elevates it above the plane of biological existence, endowing it with humanity and its own personal destiny. The same religions teach that at some special juncture in our evolutionary past the human race was "ensouled." At this particular instant, our human ancestors branched off from the larger family of life and became spiritual beings, unlike their cousins the Great Apes and lesser forms of life.

But in truth the soul does not make its debut all at once or descend from on high. There is no magic moment when it is implanted. Rather, the soul grows gradually and has an evolutionary history. It begins tentatively, in slow awakening, as the earth rouses to a dim apprehension of itself. From undifferentiated tissue, a nervous system develops, and a mind begins to form. Wishes and desires distinct from those of the womb that gave it birth take shape within the growing child. The process continues as from our earliest memories—from the way our parents held us when we were tired, from the games we shared with friends and playmates, and from the slowly dawning consciousness of selfhood and freedom—we gain an increasing awareness of ourselves in relation to the world, of the life around us and the life within. Rather than appearing out of nowhere, the soul is assembled from the all the ordinary stuff of experience. Sometimes it must be acquired painfully and through long experience.

This way of being "ensouled" is entirely natural. The whole living earth excites the child's imagination and becomes an organic part of the young person's inner world. "There was a child went forth every day," Walt Whitman wrote, "and the first object he look'd upon, that object he became. . . .

> The early lilacs became part of this child,
> And grass and white and red morning-glories, and
>   white and red clover, and the song of the
>   phoebe-bird,
> And the Third-month lambs and the sow's pink-
>   faint litter, and the mare's foal and the cow's calf,
> And the noisy brood of the barnyard or the mire by
>   the pond-side,
> And the fish suspending themselves so curiously
>   below there, and the beautiful curious liquid,
> And the water-plants with their graceful flat heads,
>   all became part of him.

That child exists in each one of us, absorbing the sights and sounds of nature, incorporating them into who we are. If by soul we mean our sense of self, our identity as particular persons, then our souls are interwoven with those of other living beings.

My own children remind me that becoming human is a continuous unfolding. One evening my son was playing with his toys in the tub when suddenly something caught his eye. Reflected in the chrome fixture encircling the water faucet was his own image. He looked at me, then back at his reflection. With a happy smile of self-recognition, he called out his own name, "Noah."

Every parent knows that mirrors make fine toys. Infants enjoy gazing into the parallel universe of the looking glass. My wife and I often hold our children up to the mirror, especially if they are dressed in a special outfit, and ask, "Who's that handsome boy?" or "Who's that pretty girl?" Noah, at two and a half, can recognize himself in the glass and reaches up to feel the red hat he's wearing that he sees reflected in the mirror. Holly, a year younger, stares curiously at the image of a fair-haired little girl in the glass. She points her finger toward the mirror and says "baby," but she does not yet recognize the image there as her own.

At some stage in their development, children gain a sense of self. They become aware of their own distinctive being and identity. A child is eventually able to express this awareness verbally with the words "I," "me," and "mine." With children too young to talk, mirrors are one of the tools psychologists use to measure this growing sense of selfhood.

The age at which children begin to recognize themselves can vary, and findings differ among various psychologists. At six months babies are likely to treat their mirror images as playmates and will reach out to touch their new friends. Slightly older children begin to grasp the reflective properties of a mirrored surface; if another person appears in the looking glass, the child turns away from, not toward, the mirror to see who has entered the room. At about two years of age self-recognition takes place. If a mother surreptitiously puts a dot of rouge on the tip of her toddler's nose, and the youngster is then placed before a mirror, the child's hand reaches out not to the mirror but to his or her own face to investigate the strange crimson mark.

The child's development retraces evolutionary development in this case. Fish, birds, and many mammals regard a mirrored image as another member of their own species and may curiously investigate the animal they see before them. Some fish will attack their own reflections (a male responds to the image as a competing male). Monkeys, on the other hand, appear to understand that shiny surfaces reflect, and they use mirrors to look at objects indirectly. They do not, however, recognize themselves. Beside human beings, only members of the Great Apes—chimpanzees, orangutans, and gorillas—have the capacity for self-recognition. A chimp whose face has been marked with red dye will, like a human child, direct its attention and curiosity not to the image seen in the mirror but to its own features. Indeed, chimpanzees will spend hours in front of the glass, brushing their teeth, making faces, and contemplating their own appearance.

When chimpanzees that have been cross-fostered— reared within a human family and treated like human sons or daughters—look into the mirror, what do they see? Beings much like their adoptive parents, no doubt. Asked to sort a stack of photographs into two piles, human and animal, such an ape will invariably put his or her own snapshot into the human category. Why not? A chimpanzees's self-concept is shaped by his or her surroundings. Growing up in a suburb rather than a rainforest or a zoo, cross-fostered chimps see themselves not as wild animals but rather as individuals who happen to enjoy bananas (a taste that is probably innate) but also like a bowl of milk and Cheerios to go with them (appetites that are surely acquired). The soul—the "I" that each of us calls "me"—emerges from these biological and social origins.

We gain our awareness of self by seeing our own images reflected in the world around us, and there are many kinds of mirrors. To take an example that may be oversimplified, a boy learns what it is to be masculine in our culture by observing his father, and from her mother a girl learns to be what we think of as feminine. We define the "self" in relation to the "other," and the mirror reflects two ways. Thus we create our families, and our families create us. We shape our environment, and our environment shapes us. Social interactions are mirrors, culture is a mirror, and so is the natural world.

So we know ourselves as human, in part, through our relationships with the nonhuman world. Animals are one of the mirrors we use to understand ourselves, from Aristotle's "featherless biped" to Desmond Morris's "naked ape."

The question is sometimes phrased in theological language: "What is man that thou art mindful of him?" The answer given in the Psalms is that humankind has been fashioned "a little lower than the angels." Through the centuries, philosophers and scientists have tried to identify the distinctive attributes that entitle us to this enviable position. Some say that we are the political animal, or the religious animal, or the only one to use tools. It has been suggested that we are the only beings who reason, or use language, or feel shame. (Ours is the only species that blushes, wisecracked Mark Twain, "or has need to.")

None of these traits is exclusively human, however. We now know that animals also reason; they also create tools; they too use symbolic communication. Each time we claim some gift or faculty as peculiar to ourselves, we soon discover that other creatures share the same abilities. When Jane Goodall first learned that chimpanzees were making and using tools in the wild, for example, her mentor, the anthropologist Louis Leakey, observed that scientists would either have to redefine tool, redefine *Homo sapiens,* or reclassify the chimpanzee as a member of the human race. As we are increasingly coming to realize, animals can do most of the things we do and many things we can't.

What seems certain, though, is that human beings perennially compare themselves with other creatures. Like a person continually glancing into the mirror, we appear to have some nagging insecurity about our own self-image. Our loud boasts of superiority suggest not that we have any real self-confidence but that we are rather unsure of ourselves.

What distinguishes our species may be this inward anxiety. While other animals may be endowed with special gifts—acute hearing, keen eyesight, incredible speed—human beings are nothing special. This is both a biological and a moral judgment. Lack of specialization makes us highly adaptable, but it also means we have no fixed form or definite identity. Without many inborn instincts to guide us, we as human beings need models for how to live. We need a sense of our own possibilities and limits, and we find them not only in the artificial rules and restraints imposed by human society but in the lessons for living suggested by biology and the earth itself. We are the younger siblings in life's family—the perpetual neonates of the animal world. In a fundamental way we need other creatures to tell us who we are.

Animals have an inherent fascination for us. This is evident in the interest children like Noah and Holly take in other living creatures. With innocent wisdom, they appear to understand that an inchworm is a prodigy of nature and a chipmunk good grounds for astonishment. Studies show that children who are given a choice of picture books will most often select the ones that feature illustrations of other living things. A group of educators once asked more than ten thousand youngsters to vote on their favorite reading matter. The top categories that emerged were "Animals" and "Here and Now," where the typical choices in the "Here and Now" were stories like *The Accident* and *The Foundling* by Carol Carrick, realistic tales about a young boy's grief when his dog is hit by a car and the healing that takes places when he adopts a new puppy.[1] Through the lives of other creatures, both real and imaginary, children explore what it means to be human.

What will it mean for the human race if children like Noah and Holly come of age in a world bereft of other living creatures? Their growing years will be immeasurably less vivid and vibrant. Their connection with the earth will be severed, and part of their inborn potential for amazement will go uncultivated. It is not just that animals make the world more scenic or picturesque. The lives of animals are stitched into our very being—closer than our own breathing—and our souls will suffer when they are gone.

As society becomes increasingly urbanized and animals disappear from our daily lives, and as more and more species slip into the long night of extinction, our humanity will inevitably be diminished. We will become increasingly confused about who we are, and distortions of the self (egos that are chronically over-inflated or under-inflated, having no reference point in nature) may become more common. In spite of our material plenty, our inner world will be impoverished.

With the gradual disappearance of animals, we will become like children who grow up in a jungle of asphalt, or like orphans who have no family and only themselves to care for. We will have only our own fantastic creations—billboards, newspapers, and computer displays —in which to see our own image represented. Without animals, the bright, reflective qualities of the world will become inanimate and dull.

What profit do we have if we gain the whole world and lose or forfeit our own souls? The human race may survive without the chimpanzees, orangutans, and other wild creatures who share the planet. But we will have attenuated the conditions that are necessary for our own "ensoulment." We will have traded a nurturing family for a dys-spirited one. The ecology of mind will not be as vivifying and luxuriant. And when we look into the mirror there will be less and less to love.

NOTES
1. Patricia J. Cianciolo, "A Look at the Illustrations in Children's Favorite Picture Books," in *Children's Choices: Teaching with Books Children Like,* Nancy Roser, editor (New York: Putnam, 1983), p. 29.

The word "animal" comes from a Latin root that means "soul." To ancient thinkers, soul was the mysterious force that gave life and breath to the myriad of the earth's creatures. Some even spoke of a "world soul" or anima mundi *that enlivened the whole of nature. Later, theologians restricted the possession of a soul to human beings. But what is soul or spirit? Spirit is the channel through which we become conscious of the essence—the inward beauty—that dwells within another living being.*

11

Do Animals Have Souls?
What Is the Answer?

Above the first edition of his book *Daniel,* Martin Buber inscribed the words of the medieval theologian Scotus Erigena: "In a wonderful and inexpressible way God is created in his creatures."

Animals were sacred to Buber. It was through his rapport with a horse he befriended on a vist to his grandfather's country estate when he was eleven years old that the Jewish thinker first awakened to "the immense otherness of the Other."

The barn, filled with the warmth and closeness of other living beings, became a temple for the young boy, where he sensed the presence of the ineffable. When he stroked the horse's mighty mane and felt the life beneath his hand "it was as though the element of vitality itself" bordered on his skin. There was a bond of understanding between him and the mare, as if they both, without saying, knew that the other had glimpsed the same wonderful secret, or heard the same murmuring currents of being. The horse very gently raised his massive head in greeting to the child, ears flicking, then snorted quietly, "as a conspirator gives a signal meant to be recognizable only by his fellow conspirators: and I was approved."[1]

Such experiences are not uncommon. For many children, even today, it is an animal that first introduces them to the sanctities of birth and death and invites them to ponder what it means to be alive. Buber was unusual, perhaps, in never allowing the years to dim that youthful awareness of the *mysterium* that resides in other living beings. For him a creature as domestic and seemingly mundane as a housecat remained a wild and unfathomed cosmos.

"The eyes of an animal have the capacity of a great language," Buber testified, and the cat's glance bore for him a question: "Can it be that you mean me? Do you actually want that I should not merely do tricks for you? Do I concern you? Am I there for you?"[2] This instant of communication with another species, though fleeting, left a powerful impression. Such one-on-one encounters with animals were for him epiphanies: revelations into the very essence of reality.

The living world is responsive and charged with feeling, which flows like a sympathetic current between all sentient beings. Other creatures, as we have seen, can be astonishingly complex and subtle. Their emotional lives are nuanced with moods that range from grief and sadness to gaiety and glee. Their family structures and relationships can be as intricate and their bonds with one another as strong and tender as our own.

Cats and horses, as Buber realized, are creatures like ourselves, and the same is true of other animals. They are not an entirely different order of creation, but like us they have rich and spacious interiors. They contain inner landscapes: desert places and lonely canyons, cliffs of madness and rivers of serene awareness that merge in tranquil seas. They share with us a heart and mind and soul.

Animals are not our property or possessions, therefore, but our peers and fellow travelers. Like us, they have their own likes and dislikes, fears and fixations. They have plans and purposes as important to them as our plans are to us. Animals not only have biologies; they also have biographies.[3] We can appreciate the lives of animals but not appropriate them, for they have their own lives to lead.

We have been long accustomed to regard animals as things: as objects, tools, commodities, or resources. Thus we raise and slaughter them for food; we use their furs and hides for clothing and decoration; we dissect their bodies for research; we study their anatomy with detached interest. We regard other creatures as means to our own fulfillment, not as ends in themselves. One might say that we "de-humanize" animals, but this would not be accurate, since animals are not human. Rather, we "de-sacralize" animals—rob them of their holy qualities—and in the process de-humanize ourselves. For animals cannot be relegated to the status of an object. When we treat them as if they were mere biological machines—collections of conditioned reflexes—we injure both their nature and our own.

Animals are our spiritual colleagues and emotional companions. We know this to be true less through debate than through direct experience. Whatever we may say about it, people have truly mutual relationships with animals and do encounter the sacred in nonhuman form. As a child, for instance, Martin Buber often visited the stall of the dapple-grey mare that he found so stirring. He and the beast had a special affinity for each other. One day, as he stroked its side, he thought what fun he was having and became aware of his own hand. Then, with a start, he realized that the spell of camaraderie was broken. His attention had wandered from the horse itself to his own thoughts about the horse. And in that instant, he had ceased to relate to the mare as a friend and instead turned the animal into a thing: an object of gratification rather than a partner in pleasure. The horse also sensed the change. The next day when Martin returned to the stall at feeding time the horse no longer raised its head in greeting. Martin continued to pet the mare, but the relationship had changed.[4]

When we relate to another as a thing our experience is flat and lacking in depth. We never really share ourselves; we touch on surfaces alone. When we relate to others as spiritual beings, our experience opens into a "vertical dimension" that stretches toward infinity. Our world becomes softer and more intimate. We become confidantes—literally, those who come together with faith. And it is through faith—not the faith of creeds or dogmas, but the simple "animal faith" of resting in communion with each other and with the natural world of soil and sunlight—that we touch the divine.

There is an inwardness in other living beings that awakens what is innermost in ourselves. I have often marveled, for instance, watching a flock of shore birds. On an invisible cue, they simultaneously rise off the beach and into the air, then turn and bank seawards in tight formation. They are so finely coordinated and attuned in their aeronautics it is as though they share a common thought, or even a group mind, guiding their ascent. At such moments, I feel there are depths of "inner space" in nature that can never be sounded. And it is out of those same depths, in me, that awe arises as I contemplate the synchronicity of their flight.

To contain such depths is to participate in the realm of spirit. To be "made in the image of God" is to be *somebody* rather than *something*. A thing is merely the sum of its parts. Bricks and buildings are good examples of things. They can be reduced to molecules and atoms without losing much in the analysis. A *somebody*, on the other hand, is greater than the sum of its parts—people, deer, bears, and horses are examples here—and when we try to dissect or reduce them to their underlying components, we miss their very essence. Just as a symphony is more than the individual notes that compose it, a *somebody* is more than a set of behaviors or biochemical reactions.

It is impossible to define precisely what gives a great piece of music its beauty and power; when we try to define it, the magic is gone. Nor can we precisely define the soul, yet if we open our hearts we can respond to its allure. Soul is the magic of life. Soul is what gives life its sublimity and grandeur.

There is a glimmering of eternity about our lives. In the vastness of time and space, our lives are indeed small and ephemeral, yet not utterly insignificant. Our lives do matter. Because we care for one another and have feelings, because we can dream and imagine, because we are the kinds of creatures who make music and create art, we are not merely disconnected fragments of the universe but at some level reflect the beauty and splendor of the whole. And because all life shares in One Spirit, we can recognize this indwelling beauty in other creatures. Animals, like us, are microcosms. They too care and have feelings; they too dream and create; they too are adventurous and curious about their world. They too reflect the glory of the whole.

Can we open our hearts to the animals? Can we greet them as our soul mates, beings like ourselves who possess dignity and depth? To do so, we must learn to revere and respect the creatures who, like us, are part of God's beloved creation, and to cherish the amazing planet that sustains our mutual existence. We must join in a biospirituality that will acknowledge and celebrate the sacred in all life.

No longer can we discount the lives of sensitive and intelligent creatures merely because they assume non-human form. The things that make life most precious and blessed—courage and daring, conscience and compassion, imagination and originality, fantasy and play—do not belong to our kind alone.

Animals, like us, are living souls. They are not things. They are not objects. Neither are they human. Yet they mourn. They love. They dance. They suffer. They know the peaks and chasms of being.

Animals are expressions of the Mind-at-Large that suffuses our universe. With us, they share in the gifts of consciousness and life. In a wonderful and inexpressible way, therefore, God is present in all creatures.

NOTES

1. Maurice Friedman, *Martin Buber's Life and Work: Volume I, The Early Years, 1878-1923* (Detroit, MI: Wayne State University Press, 1981), p. 14.
2. Martin Buber, *I and Thou* (New York: Scribner, 1970), p. 145.
3. For this contrast of "biology" with "biography," I am indebted to Tom Regan, Professor of Religion and Philosophy at North Carolina State University.
4. Friedman, *op. cit.,* p. 15.

Nature worship may be the oldest form of human religious expression. Reverence for other living things is deep-seated in our hearts. Yet today more species than ever before are endangered and at risk of extinction. Perhaps animals can confer the wisdom required to save us from our current ecological crisis. If we can recover the knowledge that every life is sacred, we may all have a future.

12

One Earth, One Spirit
Where Do We Go from Here?

My congregation worships on Sunday morning. For others, the sabbath may fall on other days of the week. Some do not attend any formal religious services at all. But I would contend that all human beings, whether they realize it or not, have spiritual needs. Though differently expressed, the impulse to worship seems everywhere the same: to acknowledge our connection with something larger than ourselves—a power that sustains life and persists beyond all death. It is in moments of peak experience, whether of sudden insight or quiet contemplation, that we come closest to catching the meaning that eludes us in our more mundane hours.

But are we the only creatures who worship—who have episodes of feeling elevated, transported, inspired? In December of 1963, the zoologist Adriaan Kortland witnessed the following amazing tableau:

Sunset in an African rain forest. The splendor of these sunsets. A chimpanzee arrives on the scene, carrying a papaya, holding it with one hand against his loins as he walks along. This is his bedside snack. The chimp puts down the papaya. For a full fifteen minutes the animal remains as if spellbound by the spectacle of the changing colors of the dusk, and watches without moving. Then he withdraws silently into the thicket, forgetting his papaya.[1]

One can only guess what was going through the chimpanzee's mind as he stood musing on the fading light of day. Was it the soft blending of violets and magentas that stirred his imagination? Did the twilight awaken memories of other days or companions who had gone before, bringing on the long, lonely thoughts of nightfall? Was it a moment of trance or daydream or reverie?

No one can say for sure, but this almost human cousin was clearly satisfying a hunger that went beyond his immediate needs for food or sustenance. He was responding to an urge that transcended the imperatives of physical survival, an urge that can only be called spiritual. When we gaze enraptured at the setting sun; when we look up and marvel at the nighttime full of stars; when we are swept away by the roar of ocean surf or stand in meditation beneath a redwood older than any human bible, we participate in a religion as real and powerful as any on earth. What we experience at such a time—our feelings of kinship and reverence—is nothing less than the universe contemplating its own hidden depths.

This is an experience that goes beyond sectarian labels and loyalties. We all feel moved by the grandeur of Creation. I was reminded of this when I gathered not long ago with a group of other men and women who were training to be volunteers in a local hospice program. The topic of the day was spirituality, and the instructor introduced it by asking each of us to respond to the question, "What makes your spirit soar?" There were about twenty people present: Quakers, Catholics, Jews and some with no particular religious affiliation. But despite the diversity in the room, they all shared one thing. For everyone found healing and renewal in nature. Some found it in other places, too . . . in music, in scripture, in service, or in silence. But without exception, they were uplifted by the beauty of the land and sky and sea. They turned to the non-human world to refresh and restore their own sense of humanity.

It should come as no surprise that nature worship—communion with the Holy present in bird, beast, and forest—may be the original and and most elemental form of human spirituality. In the high mountain caves of Germany and Switzerland, Old Stone Age implements lie side by side with the skulls of cave bears that appear to have been arranged into symbolic patterns, remains that most scholars interpret as evidence of a cult of bear veneration, which existed among the Neanderthals who inhabited the region 70,000 years ago. Fifty thousand years later, the people of what is now Lascaux, France, created some of the world's first religious art as they decorated the ceilings of their caves with magnificent images of bison, black stag, ibex, and arctic pony.

When the Canadian government sent a delegation of Inuit to visit the famous cave paintings of Europe, the Eskimos at first seemed unable to grasp the great antiquity of the drawings, but they recognized the kindred spirit behind them They asked politely if they could meet the artists who had created such vibrant works. So while it is impossible to resconstruct the sacred cosmos of our human and proto-human ancestors, it may have had aspects in common with the thought world of people like the American Indians, who preserved a similar hunting-and-gathering existence into modern times. "Whenever in the course of the daily hunt the red hunter comes upon a scene that is strikingly beautiful or sublime," wrote Ohiyesa of the Dakota in 1911, "a black thundercloud with the rainbow's glowing arch above the mountain, a white waterfall in the heart of a green gorge, a vast prairie tinged with the blood-red of sunset—he pauses for an instant in the attitude of worship." For such people,

ONE EARTH, ONE SPIRIT

the earth and its creatures naturally possessed a sacred significance.

In attenuated form, that ancestral awe still exists in each of us. It touched something primal in me, for instance, the first time I traveled to Dead Creek, half an hour from my home in central Vermont, to watch the snow geese touch down on their annual migration from the shores of Hudson Bay to their winter homes in the Chesapeake. Eight or nine thousand of the big birds were resting and feeding in the marshes and cornfields, while others circled the sky in numbers that filled my binoculars in every direction. The spectacle of so much swirling freedom and energy lit up my brain with pure joy, so that I could only stare and marvel, and when a friend visited the area two days later to discover the geese had all departed, I felt blessed that I had an opportunity to witness a part of their yearly pilgrimmage.

The thrill we get from seeing a thousand snow geese flying south in the fall, and the more quiet enjoyment we feel watching a chickadee visit the feeder outside the kitchen window, may both be a part of our evolutionary inheritance. The Harvard biologist E.O. Wilson suggests that human beings have an inborn affinity with other creatures. Over the millenia, our nervous systems evolved through interplay with a wild environment, so we naturally respond with fascination to the animals who are members of our own family tree. They awaken memories of our own origins and help us understand our own rootedness in nature. Wilson calls this drive "biophilia," meaning the love of life, and more generally our tendency to be enthused and excited by the butterflies, blue whales, and other fabulous beasts who share the planet.

Biophilia would explain why children seem to have an almost automatic attraction to most animals. "From infancy," says Wilson, "we concentrate happily on ourselves and other organisms. We learn to distinguish life from the inanimate and move toward it like moths to a porch light."[2] In much the same way a baby goose imprints on its mother (or any nearby ethologist), children appear predisposed to fixate on things that writhe or wriggle. By the same token, abusing animals is one of the surest signs that a young person's emotional development is in serious trouble. Forming healthy relationships with other creatures seems to be a necessary part of the mental landscape for children as they grow.

Before they can be numbed and de-sensitized, young people have a keen empathy with the suffering of other species. Abundant evidence confirms this. A biographer tells us that when Abraham Lincoln was a boy, he once shot a wild turkey with his father's rifle. It was Abe's first encounter with hunting, and also his last, for he never felt like pulling the trigger after that. Clara Barton, who went on to found the American Red Cross, relates that as a young girl she once witnessed a cow being slaughtered on the family farm. At the precise moment the hired hand brought the heavy axe down on the cow's skull, Clara felt a blow to her own head and lost consciousness. When she woke up, she became a vegetarian and never willingly ate meat again. What such stories suggest is that compassion is not a quality that needs to be learned. Rather, it's cruelty that must be cultivated and encouraged, as tender feelings are slowly calloused and hardened.

Over time, however, most of us lose our innate sympathy. From parents and elders, from church and school, we learn the lesson that only one species on earth really matters and that people who care about animals are sentimental, irrational, or misinformed. Animals, we are told, have no feelings. They have no souls. They have no significance in and of themselves but exist only to serve and satify human wishes. We deny the inner wisdom we possessed as children. We suppress our intuitive feelings of reverence and relatedness. And this denial is what enables us to use and exploit animals as research tools, commodities, and resources. It explains how so many people accept as "normal" a diet and lifestyle that demands the needless suffering of countless other creatures.

Learning to treat other beings with respect is especially critical at this moment when the earth itself seems to be danger. For the way we relate to other animals is a vital indicator of our attitude toward the natural world in general. Unless we can open our hearts to the animals who are so much like ourselves, how can we hope to respond with passion to problems like destruction of the rainforests or depletion of the ozone? Statistics on extinction are plentiful. Those who know say that if present trends continue, millions of species—up to a quarter of all those presently living— will be lost within the next thirty years. A newspaper reported that Monarch Butterflies, those colorful visitors to our summer gardens, may be endangered because of destruction of their winter home in the forests of southern Mexico. Like the snow geese I saw last fall, these animals will be here one day and gone the next. But this time, of course, they will have vanished utterly, never to return.

The concept of extinction, like the notion of eternity or "forever," is not one we understand easily. It goes beyond the problem of mere mortality. Most of us know from personal experience what it means to die. We have mourned for pets or friends or family members. Indeed, human beings are not the only animals who suffer or struggle inwardly when a loved one leaves the world. Like elephants, who bury their dead, badgers also seem to ritualize their parting. They not only entomb the bodies of the deceased in the side tunnels of their setts or burrows but have also been known to dig holes in the open fields, where they drag and then heap soil over the forms of their lifeless companions.[3] Grief is a natural reaction, common to many species; a mother seal sheds tears that are physiologically much like ours when her pup is clubbed by hunters.

Our biology guides us in how to feel and what to do when facing death, but the extermination of a species is something else entirely, since it means not just the demise of every living representative of the tribe but of all unborn generations as well. Death is a part of life and the corollary of birth, whereas extinction means the annihilation of life and the end of birth. Imagining what that means when multiplied a million-fold is literally beyond our grasp. We lack the neural equipment to respond to threats that seem too imponderable and far removed from immediate experience.

At the same time, the story of one animal, like Keiko, the real-life killer whale who starred in the movie *Free Willy*, can grasp the attention of the entire world. With the help of school children who saved their pennies and the committed hard work of many caring adults, Keiko was rescued from the tiny tank in a Mexican aquarium where he had spent most of his life and transported to a marine mammal rehabilitation facility in Oregon. His next move will be closer to his birthwaters near Klettsvik Bay, Iceland, where he will live in a special open-sea containment area, hearing and communicating with other members of his species for the first time in nineteen years. With luck, Keiko will eventually be reunited with his family. When that day comes, thousands of fans and supporters will be cheering.

One animal in pain or distress—be it a dolphin, a dog, or a wounded bird—is something we can understand viscerally. We respond with the urgency that's needed. This in itself seems to be part of our instinctive repetoire. As Great Apes, we have the capacity to care for the sick and injured, not only of our own species but others as well. When a three-year-old boy managed to climb the guard rail and tumble down two flights of concrete into the enclosure for gorillas at the Brookfield Zoo near Chicago, knocking himself unconscious, the immediate response of one of the animals, Binti, was to approach the child and cradle him in both arms. With her own eighteen-month-old infant clinging to her back, the gorilla then carried the toddler to the nearest exit, where paramedics were able to retrieve and then revive the injured child. Why should we be surprised? Binti (whose name in Swahili means "Daughter of Sunlight") was helping a fellow primate, a being much like herself, with whom she shared a common capacity for nurturing and love.

We primates exhibit our share of aggression, of course, but under the right circumstances we can also be compassionate creatures. In one rather sadistic experiment, rhesus monkeys (sometimes called macaques) were given an opportunity to receive food by delivering an electric jolt to another animal that could be seen in restraints through a one-way mirror.[4] Unless he pulled a chain that delivered a painful shock to his helpless lab mate, the monkey received no rations. Under these conditions, eighty-seven percent of the animals turned out to be conscientious objectors. They refused to shock and torment their helpless companions. One monkey went without food for two weeks rather than succumb to such deliberate cruelty.

Although humans are not always so kind, we too can be affected by the suffering of others. The outpouring of concern that moved hundreds of volunteers to help hand-wash the oil-soaked birds who were victims of the Exxon Valdez oil spill in Alaska is the kind of energy we need to harness on a permanent basis. The crusade for animal rights intersects the campaign to save the earth precisely at the point where we have the ability to care.

The environmental crisis is above all a spiritual crisis. And it will not be resolved until we can recapture the knowledge we seem to have lost: that we are not separate from the web of life but merely one strand in the design. Animals may be the teachers who can help us recover that sense of connection. If we let them, they can touch our hearts. If we look into their eyes, we can see the grief and joy that are a reflection of our own humanity. If we expand the circle of our awareness, we will realize that we are not the only species on this planet that glories in the majesty of a sunset, or that dances, like the chimps of Gombe, to welcome the lifegiving moisture of a summer shower.[5] For even within the chimpanzee there is a principle that celebrates, that worships, that touches on the transcendent. In the animal as in the human there is a spirit that responds and corresponds to the Great Spirit, whose life and breath are in every being.

The unity of life is an immemorial teaching, recorded in many times and differing spiritual traditions:

"Ask now the beasts and they shall teach thee," we read in the Bible, "and the fowls of the air, and they shall teach thee. Or speak to the earth, and it shall teach thee, and the fishes of the earth shall declare unto thee."

Says the Koran, holy book of the Moslems, "There is not an animal on earth, nor a flying creature flying on two wings, but they are peoples like unto you."

"The greatness of a nation and its moral progress," observed the great Hindu teacher Mahatma Gandhi, "can be measured by the way in which its animals are treated."

In recovering the primordial knowledge that all life is sacred, we may not only manage to save our world, we might save our own souls as well. In learning how to peacefully co-exist with other species, we might also find peace within.

NOTES
1. Elisabeth Mann Borgese, *The Language Barrier: Beasts and Men*
    (New York: Holt, Rinehart and Winston, 1965), p. 140.
2. E.O. Wilson, *Biophilia* (Cambridge, Massachusetts: Harvard
    University Press, 1984), p. 1.
3. Ernest Neal, *Badgers* (Poole, Dorset: Blanford Press, 1977),
    p. 217.
4. Jules Masserman, Stanley Wechkin, and William Terris,
    "'Altruistic' Behavior in Rhesus Monkeys," *The American
    Journal of Psychiatry*, vol. 121 (1964), pp.585-585.
5. Jane Van-Lawick Goodall, *In the Shadow of Man* (New York:
    Dell Publishing Company, Inc., 1971), pp. 66-67.

We also recommend Gary Kowalski's
marvelous book, **Goodbye, Friend**
which helps us deal with the loss
of a beloved animal friend.

For pet lovers, the loss of a cherished pet ranks
almost as high as the loss of a close family
member in terms of grief experienced. In
Goodbye, Friend, Gary Kowalski takes you on a
journey of healing, offering warmth, guidance,
and practical advice on how to deal effectively
with death by honoring your animal companion's life. A superb and comforting book for
both adults and children.

*"Uplifting, comforting, spiritual. If you have an elderly or ailing animal companion, please read
this book!"*
Alex Pacheco, Chairman & Co-Founder
People for the Ethical Treatment of Animals

*"This wonderful book is the best guide I know of that can help us deal with the death of our
animal companions whom the more we love the more we will grieve."*
Dr. Michael W. Fox, Vice President
The Humane Society of the United States
author, *The Boundless Circle*

"Saying goodbye to a pet soul-mate is something we dread but must inevitably accept. Goodbye,
Friend *offers answers that are woven into a tapestry of care, compassion and unconditional love for
the pets with whom we've shared our hearts and homes. Then, we can become much more than our
pet's best friend—we can become healers, teachers and angels for our friends and family when they,
too, lose a beloved pet."*
Marty Becker, DVM
co-author, *Chicken Soup for the Pet Lover's Soul*

*"The death of a beloved pet is one of the hardest things to bear. This insightful and compassionate
book will help readers accept the grief and move on in their lives."*
Phillip Gonzalez
author, *The Dog Who Rescues Cats*